Praise For Time–*in* Parenting

Time–in is a valuable concept that parents will want to explore as a part of their positive parenting repertoire.

Fran Fearnly
Editor-in-Chief, *Today's Parent*

Discipline means teaching children how to succeed in life and Dr. Weininger's book certainly helps parents give their children the tools they need. The home is the first society that children are exposed to, where they learn how to understand their feelings and what is expected of them. This emotional and social foundation is the basis from which children experience future successes. This book shows parents how to use time–in to help their children handle strong emotions. An important part of discipline is achieving a parenting style which promotes secure and accepting family relationships. This book will help parents do so.

William Sears
Co-author of *The Baby Book*

This is a very important and most helpful book. It is important because it challenges some of our conventional wisdom about child rearing practices. It is helpful because Dr. Weininger offers parents easily applied strategies for dealing with most commonly encountered behaviour problems in early childhood, indeed in a child's life.

David Elkind
Author of *The Hurried Child*

Time-*in* Parenting

Time-*in*
Parenting

How to teach children emotional self-control, life skills, and problem solving by lending yourself and staying connected.

Otto Weininger, Ph.D.

RINASCENTE
BOOKS

Published in Canada in 2002 by
Rinascente Books Inc.
Toronto, Ontario

National Library of Canada Cataloguing in Publication
Weininger, Otto, 1929-
Time-in parenting: how to teach children emotional
self-control, life skills, and problem solving by lending
yourself and staying connected / Otto Weininger.

Includes index.
ISBN 0-9730905-0-2

1.Parenting. 2. Child rearing. 3. Emotions in children. I. Title

HQ772.W37 2002   649'.1   C2002-901902-8

Design by raining creative inc.
Printed in Canada

02 03 04   5 4 3 2 1

To Mackenzie and Cody,
my grandchildren

Table of Contents

Foreword

This is a very important and a most helpful book. It is important because it challenges some of our conventional wisdom about child rearing practices. It is helpful because Dr. Weininger offers parents easily applied strategies for dealing with all of the most commonly encountered behavior problems in early childhood.

What is so refreshing about this book is that it demonstrates over and over again, that our conventional wisdom about the value of "time-outs" is misguided. Sending a child who has misbehaved to his or her room, or to sit in a corner, presupposes that the child will use this time to reflect—*and think better of*—his or her misdeed. Yet, as Dr. Weininger makes clear, this presupposes a level of cognitive reflection that is far beyond a young child's ability. Time-outs do not teach children anything other than, perhaps, that their parents are pushing them away just when the young child needs them the most.

It is that wonderful insight that informs this book and

makes it so different from so many other parenting manuals. Dr. Weininger knows young children and understands that their behavior often results from feelings that they themselves do not understand and over which they have little control. At this age children need parents, or other adults, to teach them about their feelings and model ways of handling them. That is the rationale for Dr. Weininger's "time-in" strategies. When young children "misbehave," we help them best by being with them and assisting them in gaining mastery over the feelings that occasioned their behavior. This means we have to resist venting our own feelings by giving the child a time-out. Put simply, Dr. Weininger's philosophy is that "time-outs" are for parents, while "time-ins" are for children.

What Dr. Weininger suggests to parents is that they help children who are angry, unhappy, wilful, or upset, by sharing their own emotional control with the child. If the parent doesn't get upset at the child's behavior, if the parent sits with the child and verbalizes the child's feelings, the child is both comforted and given a sense of control. What children learn in such "time-ins" is that parents are not afraid of their emotions and know how to handle them.

This is wonderfully reassuring to the child who is given the sense that he or she can master the emotions as well. It gives children a wonderful feeling of self confidence and security. Although more demanding than "time-outs," "time-ins" are likely, for example, to handle adolescence better than children who have been reared on "time-outs."

Of the many gifts in this book, and there are many, perhaps the greatest is Dr. Weininger's insights into the thoughts and feelings of the young child. As he shows us the world from the child's perspective, we gain a fresh understanding of how young children see our behavior and what they learn from it. It is when we come to look at "time-outs" from the child's viewpoint, rather than our own, that we fully understand their folly. It is also when we look at "time-ins" from the child's viewpoint that we can truly appreciate their full value.

Dr. Weininger has done young children and their parents a very great service with this book. It deserves to be widely read and heeded.

David Elkind
Author of *The Hurried Child*

Preface

When I decided to write a small book about children for parents, I realized that although a lot of what I wanted to do sounded like common sense, some of it sounded heretical in today's world. Looking at the array of "how-to" books available for parents, I realized that parents are bombarded with information, much of it contradictory. If "experts" cannot agree, how can parents know what to do? And I wondered what the reaction would be to a book that asked for more time and thoughtfulness from parents.

This book describes variations on a single theme, which I call time-in. I believe that children develop to their greatest potential when they have parents who are able and willing to "be there" for them—physically and emotionally. It's difficult for already over-stretched parents to even contemplate yet another demand on them, but I also believe that, in the longer term, parents will be rewarded with peace of mind and pride as their children grow up.

Time-in Parenting is not "against" anything—women's rights, daycare, etc.—but is "for" the creation of positive experiences for families. Having said this, I do speak out against some child-rearing techniques, widely taught by "experts," that have negative effects on children. Parents should have the opportunity to hear the other side and make up their own minds. For example, the punishment or control technique called "Time-out" is essentially antithetical to the view expressed in this book; it is as an alternative that I offer the term "Time-in."

My children will be the first to say that I have not always met the ideal that emerges from these pages. However, I have tried to learn from my experiences with my own children and the young families with whom I have worked, so that my mistakes could lead to something positive—for myself and for others who may read this book.

I would like to thank all the parents and children who talked with me about their problems and concerns. These experiences have helped shape my understanding of them and have enabled me to write this book. And all the examples in the text are—with names changed, of course—from the real situations in which these very real people found themselves.

I would also like to thank my wife Sylvia and my family. I have learned a great deal from being a father and a grandfather. My daughter Lisa read and edited the completed manuscript. I asked Barry Cook and Dan Perlitz, my friends for many years, to read a rough draft. They willingly did so and made many helpful suggestions. I want to thank them for their friendship and generosity with their time and thoughts. I also want to thank my dear friend Joan Pinkus who drew my attention to the very special "Peanuts" cartoon strip and Andrea Knight who did such a thoughtful job of editing the text. Finally, a very special thank you to my publisher, Gillian Wallace, for her support and encouragement throughout this project, and for her invaluable contribution to the final manuscript.

Otto Weininger
Toronto, July 2002

Introduction

Time-in Parenting is a book about the heart and soul of parenting—those everyday moments and episodes at every age and stage, when children are "out of control," defiant, or overwhelmed by strong emotions, and parents are feeling frustrated and bewildered.

This is a book for ordinary and "good-enough" parents: parents who have tried to establish consistent and age-appropriate routines and expectations for their children, who have loving and nurturing homes, and who manage pretty well with their children in a variety of situations. Yet these very same parents may be confounded by babies who don't sleep through the night, toddlers who hit or clutch toys in playgroup, and children who "melt down" before dinner during the "arsenic hour."

These events are normal and occur in all families. They can be counted on to happen whether they are triggered by stress, hunger, lack of sleep, changes in routine, developmental milestones, or just the time of day. One day it might be set off by candy at the checkout counter and the next by socks that "don't feel right." How children and their parents react to these daily ups and downs will also vary with the parent's personality, mood, health, and temperament and with those of the children.

Parents care about the emotional and intellectual well-being of their children. They hope their children will be empathetic and understanding, and able to express and manage their feelings. Parents hope that their children will show initiative, independence, academic excellence, good judgment, and self-control. Parents strive to instill self-confidence and self-esteem. They start thinking about these issues at birth, and want to see evidence of emotional development as soon as possible. This puts pressure on everyone. Parents worry about spoiling their children and giving in to them, while also worrying about being consistent and predictable. Everyone feels anxious and beleaguered when emotions and behavior becomes intense. Parents are most likely to react harshly at these times.

What has happened? Parents forget that the foundation for the qualities in their children they long for is laid through everyday interactions from the moment of birth. Parents may forget that the greatest opportunities to teach self-control are during the "out-of-control" episodes. Withdrawing during a crisis (time-out) teaches withdrawal and the suppression of emotions. Time-in gives an upset child what she needs the most—her parents. It allows a parent the opportunity to turn a tantrum into a teachable moment. How we deal with difficult situations is the truest test of our character. Time-in allows us to be at our best and to help our children be at their best.

Time-in is good for children and good for parents.

Chapter One

About Time-*in*

When children are upset, out of control, rude or angry, what they need most is to be with a safe and accepting adult. They need to be with someone who is calm and non-punitive, and can recognize that anyone can get very upset at one time or other. They also need someone who can help them express these strong feelings appropriately.

Most children experience some occasions when they cannot contain their feelings—it may be at a certain time of the day or in a particular situation—and things often burst out inappropriately. They cannot "hold onto" their feelings at these times and they behave badly. At such a time, they need a parent or an adult who can help by holding and containing, and sorting out their feelings for them. They need their "original container," that is, the parent, who once held them when they were upset. Just as upset babies need to be picked up and held—"contained"—by a safe parent who will try to sooth them, so do upset children. Often, upset children do not understand their emotions and may need someone to help them think about, talk about, understand, and manage what they are feeling.

What is time-in?

1. First and foremost, time-in is holding and containing an upset child.

The process in which a parent or another adult holds and contains the feelings of an upset child is called "time-in." Time-in is the opposite of "time-out." The child needs to sit beside the parent, to be held by the parent and essentially told, "You're having a very hard time and you really don't know what to do about it. You can't handle this by yourself. I will come and sit with you and when you can, put your hand on mine."

In the first part of this message, the parent is saying the wonderful words a child wants to hear: "I am here for you." At the same time, the child is getting the ever-so-important message that it is okay to express emotions. Then, by asking the child to place a hand in the adult's hand—in his or her own time—the parent lets the child re-establish the original soothing relationship. The parent "loans" the child an adult sense of competence and confidence. By loaning himself, a parent helps a child develop the confidence to acknowledge and handle her own upset and difficult feelings.

Parents' willingness to support their children in this way actually gives children the feeling that their parent believes in them—believes they will eventually be able to handle the problem themselves. The readiness, availability, and predictability of the parent leads to the expectation that someone will be there in times of crisis. The security of knowing this yields a sense of confidence and competence in the upset child.

2. Time-in also teaches self-control

Once a child learns that his parent will be there for him and that it is okay to express emotions, then time-in gives the parent the necessary time to teach him how to handle his emotions, and to understand and control his emotions. Children need to learn these skills in order to achieve their potential. This is known as the hierarchy of emotional processing.

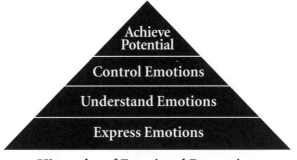

Hierarchy of Emotional Processing

Time-in provides a sense of security that enables the child to begin the task of handling difficulties. If a problem gets too big, the child knows that she can go to her parent and the parent will try not to disappoint her. She also knows that she will not disappoint her parent by asking for help. Through time-in the parent teaches the invaluable lesson, "I am here." At the same time, the parent is also teaching the child, "Fear not, for I am here." These are the foundations of self-esteem and confidence.

3. Time-in is not just for upset situations; it is for life

Time-in is a way of interacting with children in every situation. It is "listening with your eyes." It is being in the moment with your child, being connected to your child, not, for example, making dinner or reading the paper while your child talks to you. It is using your ears, your eyes, and your heart to see, hear, and be there for your child.

The enchanting book *Guess How Much I Love You* by Sam McBratney is a beautiful, strong, yet tender example of time-in parenting in ordinary situations. The book begins: "Little

Nutbrown Hare, who was going to bed, held on tight to Big Nutbrown Hare's very long ears. He wanted to be sure the Big Nutbrown Hare was listening".

Big Nutbrown Hare is there physically and emotionally for Little Nutbrown Hare. He sees with his eyes and his heart that Little Nutbrown Hare needs to express his love. He wisely sees that Little Nutbrown Hare is tired. It's almost bedtime and Big Nutbrown Hare knows what Little Nutbrown Hare needs before going to sleep. "I heard you," Big Nutbrown Hare reassures him. "I am here for you, and I love you, too." *

What upset children are feeling

When children are upset and misbehaving, we may assume that we know why. Unfortunately, often we are wrong. Even the child may not know why he is misbehaving. During a meltdown parents need to ask themselves, "What is my child feeling right now?"

When babies fuss, parents think about what might be wrong. Parents must do this with upset children, too. Only when we understand what children are feeling and why they are feeling it, can we help them channel and control the feelings appropriately.

Children need to learn not to suppress their own feelings and not to deny the feelings of others. If they are provided with opportunities to express feelings safely, children will feel encouraged to work them out. They will learn that feelings "don't kill you." As feelings become less frightening, then situations in which feelings are apt to be expressed do not have to be avoided.

Once children have the emotional security of knowing that they can express themselves, they need to be taught how to talk about what they feel, how to identify what they are feeling. To help a child do this, the parent must teach the child an effective and appropriate emotional vocabulary. From this flows under-standing. I will discuss this in more detail in Chapter 2, which also includes a "How I Feel" chart (page 38).

Talking about feelings with children – or the risk of not talking

Problems often occur because parents may not create oppor-tunities to talk about the many issues that arise during the day—we're busy. This leaves little time to find out what our children are experiencing and thinking. At the end of the day, we're tired, we have dinner to prepare, and we have many other household tasks to perform. It is hard to make time-in a priority. We think we can train children to be good and kind and understanding by telling them what we like and what we do not like about their behavior. We forget that they learn from what we model, not what we order them to do.

Time-in means not just being there for our children, but being open to talking. By talking to children we learn what is on their minds. And there is an even greater dividend: being there for children builds trust. The children learn that they can come to us whenever they need to talk, even if they don't know what to say.

On the other hand, "time-out" sends a very different message. When we are upset by something children have done, we send them out of our sight. We may be angry because they challenged our parenting. In this case, the parent may need the time-out, not the child.

We may honestly believe that by sending a child to his room he will "learn a lesson" and not behave badly again. We expect that the lesson will be learned because we send the child out of our sight; they will need us, or miss us and our activity. We think they will learn the lesson in order to avoid being sent away again in the future. Maybe we need to think again. Children may not even understand why they have been sent out of our sight, what they need to do to make amends, and how we want them to behave.

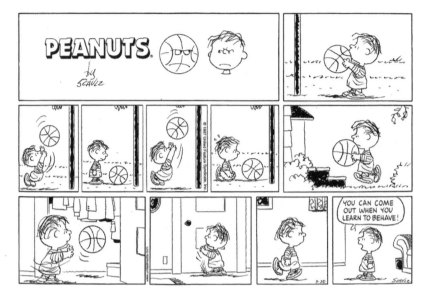

After talking with many six- to nine-year-olds, I have found that they usually say that sending them to their rooms makes them angry. What they do in the room is look around, play with toys, cry, or sleep. None of the children have said that they "think about" what "bad" thing they did. When I asked them, "Do you think about why you were sent to your room?" they say, "Sometimes." Then, without further questioning, they often add that they are "just very mad" and it takes a while to get over this feeling. They do get over their mad feelings. But they do not understand why they were sent away, other than to think "Dad was angry with me," or "Mom said I did a bad thing."

I believe we overestimate the reasoning skills of children in these situations. We forget how they think. As one child of seven said, "It was pretty bad—I kicked my train set because it wouldn't work— I think I broke it, so maybe they are mad at me for breaking the train—I don't know." Another child of six said she always got sent to her bedroom when she yelled at her sister and added,

"I don't care, I like my room— my sister is a real pest." Perhaps the parents of these children would have been better off to ask why these events happened, rather than banishing the children.

Asking why is not always easy— even adults do not usually know how to answer such a question. Getting a meaningful response requires that we talk (calmly) with the child, asking about how she is feeling, about what changed her feelings, and about what she thought before she acted out. Screaming, "Why did you do that?" at a child is not an effective way to help her talk.

The consequences of not using time-in

When we send a child away and don't explain why we did that, or when we deny our child's emotions, we abdicate responsibility as parents. We transfer the responsibility and pressure to the children, expecting them to "fix" the situation. Yet we haven't given them the tools. One of the worst consequences of abdication parenting is that the children, with their own "child-thinking" and egocentric logic assume they are "bad," that whatever has gone wrong is their fault. This "it's my fault" perspective underlines the importance of understanding what a child is thinking and feeling.

Example: The boy who (thought he) made his mother ill

A mother had been quite upset for a few weeks. She had been ill will a cold and the flu and her husband had been working unusually long hours. This meant that she had been alone with her five-year-old son a great deal of the time. As she became more upset, she tried even harder to keep their routine and do alone what both parents used to do: make dinner on time, keep the house tidy, and keep bath, bed, and story time the same. She became increasingly distressed and her cold seemed to last forever. These feelings became a prominent part of her relationship with her son. She yelled. He yelled. He became sullen, angry, and defiant. When she said he was not behaving

31

well, he said she was a bad mummy. Neither of them seemed to be able to relieve the frustration and tension.

As the impasse worsened, the boy's mother sent him to his room "until he could behave properly." He stayed there and played with his toys and seemed to "forget" to come out. His mother thought he was being defiant, but it also occurred to her that maybe he couldn't "behave properly" unless the dynamic between them changed. To her credit, she realized that he was reacting and interacting with her. And the way that she was feeling and acting was not helping the situation. She thought that rather than sending him to his room, she had better talk to him "pretty straight." She told her son that she had a bad cold, and that she was upset because she had so much to do. He responded that he was sad that she had a cold and that he could help her around the house. She also said that she became angry too easily and he said that he got angry as well, and that he got angry when she got angry. Together they decided that he could help with some jobs around the house. After a week of helping, there was a decided change in both mother and son. He developed a daily ritual of making a special lettuce sandwich (bread and lettuce only) for her. She ate every bit of that dry sandwich. He watched with great pleasure and satisfaction because he was finally able to do something that could "make her feel better and be less upset."

• • •

The boy needed his mother to be less angry, but he also needed to be able to help her in the process. As her child, he had the impression that his behavior had made her ill. Initially, nothing had happened between them to make him think differently. He imagined that he was the cause of her upset and that he was powerless to change this. He needed his mother's help to do the very thing that would return their relationship to the good one that they had had before. Because of her honesty (and humility), straight talk, and the time she spent with him, he now felt that he was good and that he could make bad things turn into good things. This could not have happened if he was sitting alone in his room.

The positive effects of presence

A child's sense of competence and sense of self is strengthened by experiencing the adult's presence. Rather than using her parent as a crutch, and searching for the adult every time she feels ready to "fall apart," the child gradually learns to handle difficulties on her own. This confidence is supported by anticipation—anticipation that her parent will be there when needed. Not only does this reduce the stress of many events for the child, but also changes her perception of situations that might become difficult. Over time, children learn what they can and cannot handle.

Example: "I have more confidence when you are near"
A ten-year-old boy who had grown up with time-in parenting came to one of his parents about a problem involving a broken window. He had accidentally broken the neighbor's window with his baseball and wanted his parent to come with him to talk to the neighbor. He said, "I'll do the talking, I just want you to be there." The parent agreed to go. As they walked over, the boy explained, "You used to sit close to me when I was angry and I could talk to you about how angry I was. I want you to be near me. It makes me feel better."

• • •

I think that what the boy was saying was that by having his parent available for time-in, he had acquired the capacity to deal with difficult and strong feelings of anger and fear. The broken window represented a new fear. While he was confident about trying to deal with it, he needed his parent as a time-in reminder while he did.

Example: The teacher who "loaned her strength"

In a second-grade classroom, the teacher had devised an unusual way of handling the beginnings of social and emotional problems. She had a finger-exerciser—a round object with protrusions that could be pushed in. She gave the exerciser to children when she noticed they were becoming upset, having difficulties with another child, or were simply bored. She told the class that she had several finger-exercisers and she talked about how important they were to her. She explained that she used them to strengthen her fingers, which helped her write and draw. She built up the importance of them to the children whenever they needed them. She added a stopwatch so they could count how many finger pressings they could do in five minutes. Whenever the teacher saw that a child was in trouble, she passed a finger-exerciser to her. The children accepted this activity and it calmed their anger or upset feelings. Classroom morale increased and the teacher noted that she was loaning the finger-exercisers much less often. As holidays or special events approached, however, the children needed the finger-exercisers more often.

• • •

I think that by offering something that was important to her, the teacher loaned the children her strength. She showed her confidence in them. "I am here," she said, which also meant, "I know you won't blow up. You will work out your feelings." She demonstrated that she was there for them, that she knew and understood them, and that she cared about them. Rather than burying their feelings, the finger-exercisers enabled the children to talk about them. After a few minutes with the exerciser, the children would go to the teacher and tell her how they had been feeling before she gave it to them and that now they could continue with their work. The children were having a time-in with an object that was—to them—a part of their teacher.

Chapter Two

About the Feelings of Children

Young children need an adult to help them understand what is "going on" inside them. Children have and express all sorts of feelings, which are often powerfully experienced and expressed as anger, hate, guilt, love, sadness, and curiosity. One of the tasks of growing up is to learn how to deal with such passing emotional storms effectively. These are very powerful inner sensations to try to understand at any age and young children cannot learn how to do this by themselves while they are upset and alone in a room. Not yet having the emotional resources to both experience and think about their feelings, when alone these emotions can become overwhelming. In fact, when forced to cope with such strong feelings alone, away from adult support, a child can even become physically ill or unusually withdrawn; either response can be potentially damaging to emotional development.

Helping children cope with strong feelings

The way we handle difficult feelings with time-in reassures children that we accept and understand their difficult times.

Many aspects of social growth have problems associated with them: rivalry, jealousy, greed, envy. Sending children away from us only creates a sense in them that, "No one understands me; no one cares about me." Unfortunately, the result is that these children will not care for themselves—they will not think they are worthwhile. And they will never master the emotions or problems that led to this experience in the first place.

Emotional growth also involves curiosity, love, ambivalence, sadness and guilt—very powerful feelings that may cause children to become as upset as they would if they were experiencing negative emotions. Children need our support and our understanding to help them recognize what they are feeling, handle these feelings, and figure out what to do about them. Our presence and acceptance enables them to realize their worth—they know through our direct involvement that we care enough about them to help them through these difficult emotions.

The "How I Feel" chart

Giving children an emotional vocabulary

Parents can help children cope with strong feelings by acknowledging emotions and by helping children identify and express their feelings. Here is a chart that helps identify some different emotions which in turn helps give children a vocabulary for expressing themselves. Parents can add to it or modify it according to a child's vocabulary.

Pleasure	Fear	Anger	Sadness
happy	scared	annoyed	like crying
joy	afraid	irritated	miserable
like smiling	anxious	frustrated	wretched
pleased	stressed	mad	unhappy
glad	jealous	like hitting	heartbroken
proud	shocked	rage	blue
delighted	guilty	furious	glum
love	terrified	defiant	low
thrilled	ashamed	resentful	gloomy

The parent-child standoff

Sometimes children can be belligerent, sarcastic, balky, or just plain defiant. The only way a child can learn about these feelings is to be with an adult who will make it safe enough for him to talk about the feelings and find alternate ways of expressing himself.

Example: When nothing else works or, "win-lose" becomes "win-win"

Jamie is a very oppositional five-year-old. If his mother says that he is to do something, Jamie says, "You can't make me," setting off a storm. He and his mother fight, and, of course, Jamie wins—he will not do whatever his mother has asked him to do. His mother becomes angry and Jamie smiles—he won! However, the victory is short-lived because Jamie is punished for winning; he has to go to his room until he "does as he's told." Jamie sits in his room for hours, looking out the window, drawing, and playing with cars. His mother was concerned because Jamie did not seem upset—he didn't seem to realize that he was being punished—and so she started putting him in a room without his toys or anything else to do. Now Jamie cries for a while in his room and his mother says to herself, "Now he knows that I mean business." What she means is, "Now I'm in control!" But this feeling soon fades; she finds that Jamie just falls asleep. The cycle repeats itself.

In desperation, Jamie's mother telephoned me for a consultation. I suggested that, instead of putting Jamie in time-out, she begin to have time-in sessions with him. She was resistant at first, but after explaining time-in and addressing her concerns about this approach, she agreed to try it for a while, saying, "Nothing else is working, anyway."

Jamie was very surprised by the change in dynamic. Rather than going through another fight for control and being told to go to his room, he and his mother sat down and she quietly held his hands and talked about the distress he must be experiencing. Within a few minutes, she was amazed to find that this calmed them both. They could even smile at each other. She told Jamie that she got upset when he was nasty to her and that there must be a reason he felt this way. Jamie answered that when he wants to do something, he "knows" that she will stop him. When his mother indicated that she would not always stop him, only when he wanted to do something dangerous, and that at other times she might even be able to help him, Jamie relaxed. He "tried on" this new approach immediately by asking to do something "ridiculous."

When his mother called again, we discussed Jamie's attempt to "outdo" his mother by asking for something over the top. Her response now is to smile and say, "That sounds pretty difficult, maybe even impossible, but let's talk about it." She no longer categorically rejects things that Jamie presents and Jamie has gradually learned that he cannot do everything. He has also learned that he can do a lot of things and has gradually found that he is "in charge of himself" up to a point. Jamie has certainly tested his mother over and over again, but within a few months, his mother stated emphatically, "He's a changed kid!" When I pointed out, "So are you," she agreed.

. . .

Jamie's mom had turned a classic win-lose situation into a win-win relationship just by being present, listening, and discussing. She modeled self-control and they both learned that they didn't have to rely on his mother's constant surveillance.

Helping children face fear and disappointment

When children are frightened or disappointed, they need time-in with their parents. I do not think any child should be told, "You've got to face your fears and conquer them alone." Young children, and often even older ones, need support and encouragement to gain confidence that they can handle irrational fears.

Example: Teddy and Mom face bugs together

Teddy, a four-year-old, is terribly frightened of bugs and so is his mother. Rather than becoming angry with him for having the same fear that she has, Teddy's mother decided to get picture books of insects, to visit museums where she and her son could see insects, and to have an insect box where they could look at bugs. Teddy is not sent to his room to get over his fear of bugs, but is learning how to confront his fear with the support of his mother. At this point, he can say that bugs will not bite him, although it is clear that he would rather not meet up with one. However, he is interested in bugs and is trying not to be afraid. Time-in with his parents is helping him with this; his mother has taught him, "I am here. Fear not."

Example: What a parent says/What a child hears

When Margit, a girl in fourth grade, was unhappy and disappointed at losing the high-jumping contest, she expressed this by pouting. Both her parents told her that if she did not stop pouting she would have to go to her room. What Margit understood from this was that they also were disappointed in her loss, maybe even angry with her, and were expressing this by sending her to her bedroom. Once again, we can't always assume that we know what our children are hearing or seeing. It may not be what we hear or see. Margit didn't understand that the issue for her parents was her pouting. Her parents didn't understand that for Margit, the issue was not knowing how to express her feelings.

By not giving Margit an opportunity to express her disappointment in herself, as well as her concern that her parents didn't love her as much because she lost, Margit's parents created a scenario in which Margit would have to "keep her feelings to herself." Margit decided that her parents wanted a "smiling idiot" and that is what she would give them. She didn't react to sad or happy events; she seemed very bland and did not express any emotions—

at least none that she thought her parents would not accept. However, she began to fail her school tests and suddenly seemed unable to understand what the teacher was telling her.

Margit did try to give her parents a "smiling idiot." In family therapy meetings, she talked about the contest and how she felt. The therapist then helped her parents give Margit permission to talk to them about her worries and concerns. Margit suggested that it would be better for all of them if she could "just tell them" how she felt and if they would "just listen and stop telling her how to feel." Fortunately, her parents recognized that when Margit was experiencing the serious disappointment most acutely, it would have been so much wiser to listen to their daughter and not behave as if her failure meant their failure. They began to recognize that sending her away from them was not what she needed. On the contrary, she needed to be with them to explore why she had failed, how she felt, and what she could do in the future to try to win. Time-in with her parents would have saved Margit and her family considerable anxiety.

Helping children express sadness

Many parents have considerable difficulty allowing their children to express their sad feelings. These include their feelings of grief and mourning over the loss of a friend or family member (including a pet), or even when something that they considered precious is lost, like a scarf or a baseball. Parents sometimes do not recognize the importance of acknowledging their own grief and mourning and try to deny it. It is as if what happened was not very important in their lives. Yet the denial of these feelings creates foundations for a lifelong sense that "something is missing"; "something just feels wrong"; "I don't know how to put it, but I feel like a piece of me is missing." These are some of the remarks adults make when they are denying loss.

Loss is a prominent feature in children's lives. They are usually concerned that their parents will be there for them and that they will not be alone. All too often children think that if they are alone, it must be because they have been "bad." Of course, when the parents return, the child is pleased and begins to feel reassured. But even this process takes a while.

Example: Using time-in to soothe a frightened baby

A six-month-old baby, after his first separation from his mother, started to cry when she returned. His mother went to pick him up, but stopped and, instead, talked quietly to him. She told him she was home, that she loved him, and that he was safe. She repeated these words for a few seconds and, as he calmed down, she then picked him up; he looked so very pleased. Once again, he had his beloved mommy.

• • •

By recognizing that her baby was upset and talking to him, rather than just picking him up, this mother was able to give her baby time-in. She enabled her baby to express his feelings directly to her. She did not just try to block them out because they hurt her as well. She allowed her baby to cry, accepted his cry, and then held him.

Most parents in similar circumstances will hold their babies immediately. But that is like trying to keep their baby's emotions away from them, helping the parents to deny these strong feelings. This mother, by talking to her baby, essentially recognized the need he had at that moment to have his feelings contained—safely acknowledged—and not denied. This enabled him to respond to his mother without mixing his feelings of anger toward and love for her for having left and returned—something he was not emotionally ready to do. His mother held the anger while her baby expressed the love and joy. Later, when he is more mature, the child will be able to deal with the anger that he always feels when he is left alone.

What a parent can do for an angry child

Anger is a powerful and often frightening emotion that all children experience, from the hungry newborn to the door-slamming adolescent. Children are angry a lot of the time. Sometimes we know they are angry, when they shout or hit, and sometimes we do not know how angry they are.

Anger is healthy and normal. It is derived from healthy aggression—a life force necessary for our very survival. Without it we could not surmount developmental obstacles, become independent, or experience life with vigor and creativity. It can be a sign of health and hope.

Many situations evoke anger in children—including the frustrations of growing, changing, and daily living. Learning to walk, starting school, going to bed, and taking vacations are all examples of events during which children might experience anger and show it in a variety of ways, from hitting or shouting, to dawdling or misbehaving.

Anger is a complex emotion for children and for adults. It is especially so for children whose thoughts are normally filled with monsters and other dangerous creatures. Angry encounters between parents and children are fraught with anticipation, fear of retaliation, and guilt. I remind parents, once again, don't assume that you know what your child is thinking or feeling. And don't forget that, being egocentric, a child may assume that "it is my fault" and that "I am bad."

Children are often afraid of their own anger. They have not yet learned to distinguish between their own angry thoughts and the destruction they think they can inflict on their parents through these thoughts. They feel omnipotent and this omnipotence, as well as the omnipotence they believe their parents have, terrifies them. Children worry that their angry thoughts will damage or destroy their parents, or that these thoughts will provoke the parents to be angry with them.

When children anticipate their parents' anger as a consequence of their own angry feelings, they may become even angrier and misbehave more, even if there is no basis in reality for their perception. It's as if their increased anger is an attempt to cope with the anger that they already can't cope with. As if the anger will "get rid" of the earlier, frustrating anger. All this does is make the child terrified and the ever-escalating anger finally culminates in a temper tantrum in which no one can touch her or even come close to her. She is "too dangerous" now and even touching her parent could destroy the parent—or so some children have told me after an outburst, when we sat quietly and talked. At this point, children may misinterpret benign parental remarks and behavior as proof of, and then attacks on, their "badness." When this happens bewildered parents sometimes end up really getting angry!

It is most tempting to use time-out when children are angry because their anger stirs up anger we have inside us. As scary as this anger is for us, it is even more frightening to the child. We want them, and our anger, in control and "out-of-sight." When the child is out of sight, the anger is out of sight and the parent can calm down. However, all that I think we have done in this situation is project our anger onto the child's anger, so sending both angers away relieves us of both our own anger and that of the child. The child, however, is left to cope alone with a double load of anger.

This is the time when children most need to see that we have not been damaged or destroyed by their rage. They need our calmness and our patience to demonstrate that we will not allow them to damage themselves. We have to lend them our control and our confidence to help them regain control. We have to show them and tell them these things. We have to repeat that we love them, even while they are screaming, "I hate you." Someone has to be the adult. I think that it should be the parent.

A child who is left alone with rage is not reassured that we, or they, are unharmed. We force them to stifle their original feelings and substitute anxiety, fear, and still more anger and resentment toward us for sending them away. Fear of desertion and of withdrawal of love are more powerful weapons than their instigating rage—no wonder the anger appears to go away so quickly. It has not gone away, but has merely been superseded by other feelings that are even more powerful. It will remain inside and re-emerge in other ways.

Sending children away to get control of their anger perpetuates the feeling of "badness" inside them and leads them to view their parents as "bad" because they could not help them with these strong feelings. Chances are they were already not feeling very good about themselves before the outburst and the isolation just serves to confirm in their own minds that they were right. Parents will recognize the angry child who refuses comfort or hurls a favorite toy across the room when upset. And most parents have been told at one time or another that their child is "so good at school. We never see a tantrum here." Children are more likely to direct their anger and frustration toward people they expect to be close to them, and from whom they need containment. They direct their anger at the person(s) they believe can meet their needs and keep them safe. To send them away for "time-out" can be experienced by the child as a complete failure of understanding. At these moments children need our quiet physical presence to transform the badness that they imagine in themselves—and in us—and then transfer to the toy that they throw against the wall. It is at such times that parents adapt themselves to the developing child's emotional needs.

It is often confusing to parents when they experience anger from their children on holidays, special events, or birthdays. But this anger often stems from a child's feeling that he has taken "too much" from his parents, who will therefore be angry with him. This is especially true for a child whose parent, even casually, remarks how tiring all the work for the party has been. Then the child is sure that he took too much, asked for too much, and has made his parent tired, if not upset.

On the other hand, when children feel that they haven't got "enough"—regardless of how much they did get—they can be angry with others whom they perceive to have "more" than they do. This often underlies fights between siblings or squabbles about toys at pre-school. This jealousy is normal and healthy, and even shows the child's capacity to love. Usually, children who have experienced jealousy, and just about all do, come to terms with it when they realize their parents do love them.

Jealousy can create strong feelings of love and hate, which can be confusing to all involved. The "hate" may be displayed as anger. "Containing" the child, making the child feel safe with this abundant anger helps him realize that things can be put right. Healthy jealousy—that is, jealousy that doesn't arouse anger—becomes healthy ambition and competition. By staying with children at these times, and supporting their emotions, parents and teachers are, in fact, able to give the children the very thing they most desire—more of themselves. This is always what children want most, especially when they are angry. They need their parents to listen to them with their ears and eyes. And with their hearts.

Time-in to set things right

When children express anger, a very important element is their need to set things right, not through an artificial "I'm sorry," but through doing something that relieves the intensity of the anger and the and anxiety associated with it. During, or following, a time-in for an angry outburst, it is helpful to share a short and simple task or activity. Reading a story, having a snack, making dinner, doing a puzzle, or drawing a picture are all useful strategies for helping children and parents restore their relationship. When children feel that they cannot "set things right" they get even angrier. This will certainly happen if they are sent to their room.

For a child, setting things right means doing something nice for the parent whom the child thinks he has hurt. So the child makes a drawing and gives it to his parent, or gives his parent a big hug and kiss, or tells his parent. "I love you." This reparative act settles things and now the child knows that things are back on the loving, caring path.

Why anger may feel safer than confusion

The paradox children present to us is that even when they know they are angry, they may recognize this anger as a way to avoid feeling confused. One boy said, "I know what I'm doing, even if it's bad." He was saying that it is better to know what you are doing than to become confused. Confusion sets in when a situation or feelings cannot be dealt with directly and anger helps to avoid this confusion. As one eight-year-old girl said, "I can't read the book, I don't know how to read, and, I don't care." She is very angry and she's afraid she might find out by reading what it is that she is so angry about—she is angry at herself for not being able to read. Being angry helps to avoid the confusion she might experience if she tried to decode all those letters on the page.

The anger a child feels not only avoids confusion, it can provide its own justification. As so many children have said, "I have a right to be angry because I was sent to my room." Having been sent to her room, the child feels rejected. She now does not have to worry about possible rejection—she has been rejected. Now her own anger is justified and no longer represents a threat; from her perspective, her rejection has given her every reason to feel angry. Now she can say, "Because I'm so angry, I don't feel confused. I know I'm angry and I know why."

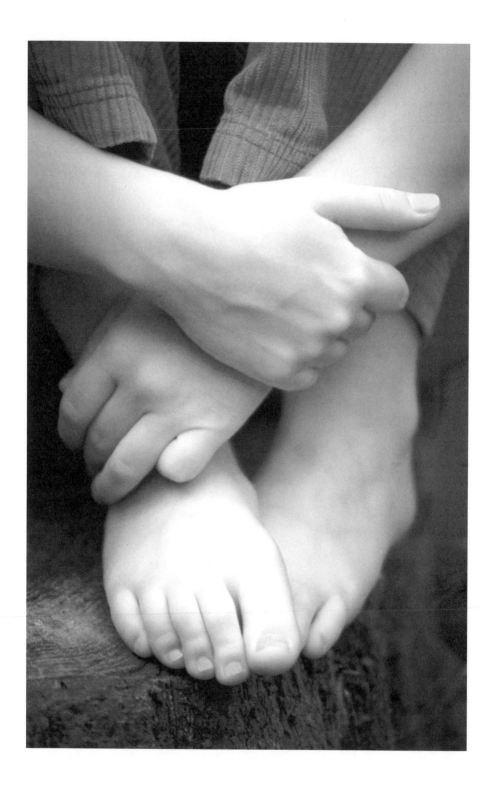

Chapter Three

More About Time-out

I have often heard parents telling their young children, "You've been very naughty, you have to go to your room until you behave properly" or "That's a very bad thing that you've done, you must not hit anyone. You go to your room until I call you to come out." I have also heard some parents give another version of this when they say, "We can't allow you to behave in such a rude way; you go to your room and when you think you can behave properly then come back to play." Parents tend to respond badly to children's refusal to do things the parents' way—for example, to eat their meals at the right time, to do their homework, to finish their chores before they watch TV, and even, as silly as this might sound, to feel good and be okay.

For many parents, these behaviors on the part of their children require punishment and the most common punishment is, "You go to your room and stay there until you learn how to behave." But if we can stand back and think about this, it must sound somewhat absurd to the child because it assumes that, at any age, we learn by ourselves and do not need others to help us. It assumes that we already somehow know the "right" way to do things and can simply go to our room and "tune into" the right way. Again, it appears to the child, we do not need anyone to help us to do this.

Too often, we operate on the premise that a "rude" child who is sent to his room to think about things, will be able to think about his behavior and, recognizing that it is rude, actually know what to do about it. However, I do not believe that children of two, three, four, five, or even six are able to perform such thinking tasks because they do not yet have the reflective skills to do so.

Sometimes children do amaze us and in our presence tell us that they will "be nice" and not behave like Tom or Suzie. They impress us because they seem to be able to recognize what is not acceptable to us. As a result, we imagine they can think about such things when they are by themselves. However, young children need our presence to make the jump from thinking out loud about things while they are with us, to thinking about things alone. In order to translate their thoughts into changed behaviors, they need our presence even more.

Parents who tell a child to go to his room until they tell him when to come out are actually making an amazing assumption that they know how long it will take him to recognize his transgression. In fact, I think that the amount of time a child is left in his room depends more on the parent's level of guilt and anger. The greater the anger, the longer the child will have to stay in his room—the greater the parent's guilt, the less time he will have to spend alone.

Telling children to stay in their room as long as they need to, or leaving it up to children to decide how long they are to remain there, are not useful ways of helping children understand the consequences of their actions. This technique does not help children develop a way of judging whether they should or should not do or say a certain thing. Rather than being helpful to young children, time-out serves the parents—who, for one reason or another, need to have their child out of sight at that particular time. Time-out is not a method of discipline; it is a punishment that deprives a child of the very relationship that he needs at the time the punishment is given.

Do we really need to punish children?

There are so many times when parents and caregivers seem to feel that in order for a child to develop "effectively" or "properly" or even to become a decent person, the child needs to be punished. The punishment may take the form of a verbal scolding, or of depriving the child of something that she likes, or slapping or hitting. The punishment that is considered to be most "politically correct" is to isolate the child by sending her to her bedroom, or to a closet, or to the empty basement, or having her stand at the end of the room, not making a sound. Usually the parents say they will let the child know when she can return; other parents, as I have noted, send a child to her room, telling her to stay there until she thinks that she can behave properly. Unfortunately, some adults do not even tell the child why she is being sent to her room. But even those who do, make that remarkable assumption that the child is capable—all alone by herself—of correcting an "adult-viewed wrong".

Many children with whom I have spoken do not have any idea of why they are being sent to their room and when pressed for an answer say, "Because Mom (or Dad) was mad at me" or "I made them mad" or "They say I'm bad and have to learn my lesson." Essentially, these represent many variations on the theme of being bad simply for making someone angry. I think it is extremely difficult for children to handle a major issue such as being bad and making others angry all by themselves. More often than not, they tell me that when they have gone to their room or the basement to be alone, they play quietly, they don't know what to do, and that they cry or they think they should be dead. They think they have just become a nuisance, that they should be sent away. Again, there is a constant theme of "I'm bad and must be punished."

Not one of the children I spoke to talked about how they would correct their behavior. They did say, "I won't get you mad at me anymore," "I won't take the apple without asking anymore," "I won't wet my pants anymore," and on and on. They identify the problem, but they do not know what to do other than say they will not do it any more.

Of course, this sort of punishment simply asks for just this sort of response. There is certainly no opportunity for the child to think through the issue—she cannot do this by herself. She needs someone, an adult who cares for her, to help her understand what she has done wrong. As the child talks about what has happened, helped by her parent to describe the event, she gains the experience of not only realizing that parents are people she can talk with, but they are also helpful in clearing up confusion, anxiety, and doubts about herself, about her social behavior, and about her acceptability to her parents. This is time-in—a time when the child has the opportunity of being with parents in times of difficulties, pain, trouble, and hurt. This is a gift that a parent gives a child for life. The child has learned that her parent is there for her when she needs it. In the process, she will also have learned to be there for her children or for others in the future.

Happy feelings versus sad feelings

It is interesting that when children are experiencing happy feelings we want them to be with us and to share their happiness with us. Why, so often, can we not bear to have our children with us when they are unhappy? Is it that we are frightened by these feelings? Do they make us feel like inadequate parents? Is this why we send them away to their rooms, from where we expect they will emerge quiet and remorseful, when they are really quiet and inwardly angry?

Example: Punishing "bad" feelings

When seven-year-old Lana was sent to her room because she refused to eat her meal, her parents thought that this would "show her who's boss" and "she'd learn to eat her dinner at dinnertime." But all that this time-out accomplished was to make Lana very resentful of her parents and drive her resentfulness "underground." During her play psychotherapy sessions, Lana said she really "hated" her parents. She said, "They don't know how I feel—they just want me to do things their way, they don't care about my way."

• • •

Driving Lana's feelings underground did not help her fussiness at the dinner table. She would eat her meals at the right time—but about five minutes after finishing her meal, she would vomit. Lana was rejecting her parents' control and getting rid of what they gave her. It was her vomiting symptom that brought her into play psychotherapy.

The negative effects of rejection

When the parent is unavailable, that is, when the parent insists on sending the child to his room for a "cooling-off time," the child does not experience a sense of parental strength. The child experiences the adult as a dictator. Children with unavailable parents are more apt to be angry children, even hyper-angry children, seeing danger in too many situations and reacting to these with defensive anger. This anger is actually the child's most effective way of stopping himself from becoming dejected, depressed, and withdrawn. These depressive feelings set in because most children view being sent away to "cool-off" as a rejection. From their perspective, they were so bad that they had to be sent away. The anger acts to prevent a sense of depression and, in this sense, is a good sign—in that the child has not yet given up hope of getting a positive response from his environment.

Example: What do children really learn from time-out?

One parent felt that she had the right answer for situations in which her children were "out of control"—that is, when they were very bad, disobedient, discourteous, or not quiet. She sent them to their bedrooms and locked their doors. She told them that they had to stay in their rooms for a specific length of time and set an alarm clock for that period of time. When the alarm rang, she unlocked the doors and told the children that they could come out, as long as they were prepared to "behave properly." She soon discovered that she didn't even have to lock the doors. When the alarm rang, the children didn't come out of their rooms—she had to go and tell them to come out. Even then, they often didn't want to leave their rooms. This parent saw this as evidence that she had "conquered" all her children's behavioral problems, that they now knew they had to behave or they would be sent to their rooms. She saw the children's desire to stay in their rooms as evidence that her children knew how long it took them to feel better and be ready to rejoin the family. She felt that her children had learned something positive.

· · ·

On the contrary, I think the children learned to avoid their mother. Rather than learning how to handle their problems, they had learned how to withdraw in the face of difficulties. I am very concerned about what will happen to these children when they reach adolescence. I predict that they will not stay in their rooms then; instead, they will run away from home. Home has not been a safe understanding place; it has been a rejecting place without the support and security that children need.

These children will be unable to feel that their home will have anything to offer when their needs and feelings are especially intense, as they will be when they begin to deal with all those difficult issues that emerge at around the time of adolescence.

How it feels to be sent to your room

I spoke to some young children about being sent to their rooms when they misbehaved. At first they seemed to say that going to their rooms was not such a bad idea because they had all their toys there and could play with them. However, one six-year-old girl said that when her parents saw that she was playing with her blocks, they told her she had to sit and think about why she was in her room. Another seven-year-old girl said, "I try to think of what it is and then I become very confused—I don't know what to think about and I seem to just even forget where I am." A seven-year-old boy added that he knows why he is in his room, but he doesn't care because, "I just do what I want to." Then he added, "They don't care anyway—they just want me to be good all the time."

The three children said that they usually felt sad when they went to their rooms "that way," but that they would get over their sad feelings. Being sent to their rooms was not a bad idea—it was, they said, "So we would learn a lesson." They mentioned again that it was not a bad idea, and when I pursued this, they said that their parents told them that they were not going to spank them for being bad, they were being sent to their room to learn how "to behave properly." I think the notion that "it's not a bad idea" came from the children's attempt to interpret and understand their parents' way of teaching them and that—from the child's point of view—it's better to go to your room than to be spanked.

As they talked about their sense of "badness," the children spoke about becoming better kids, about learning how "to obey your adults." They seemed so concerned with trying to please and with looking at themselves as bad or wrong. Perhaps, in their eyes, they had misbehaved and transgressed some spoken or unspoken law of the family. Nevertheless, sending them to their rooms only taught them that aggression, or emotional difficulty, is never tolerable. Unless you behave properly all the time, you are not acceptable. I believe that this robs children of the opportunity to explore various potentials of their own intelligence, personality, and creativity. It does not encourage or allow children to take risks, to try out something that may not be entirely successful, or even to make a mess and be noisy.

Different children's responses to isolation

Most parents can attest to the different reactions that children have to being punished with isolation. One child, accused and sent to her room because she was angry, remains angry. A very different reaction occurs in another child, who having been sent to her room for being angry, becomes docile. The latter child seems to become a much younger child, to regress and behave immaturely. Parents have described such reactions as, "She didn't seem to know what time it was even though she could read time." Or, "He started to burp like he did when he was a small baby." Or, "She said she couldn't tie her shoe laces; she needed our help— and she's been tying shoe laces for two years now." Another reaction that children have when trying to control their angry feelings is to become unusually clean, neat, and tidy. Being unusually tidy is their way of trying to make sure that order prevails. Since they cannot display their anger, the way to avoid disorder and confusion is to be orderly and neat.

Putting a child in isolation, even for a short period of time, does not help her develop a sense of confidence about how to handle strong feelings. Rather, what this does is tell her, "We cannot tolerate you when you are upset." It does not give the child the opportunity to work through feelings that are challenging and intense at that moment, forcing the child (who is able) to "sit on" the feelings—to suppress, disregard, or deny them—but not to work through them. The process of working the emotions through can only be accomplished with another person who values and trusts that the child has the resources and potential to cope with strong feelings.

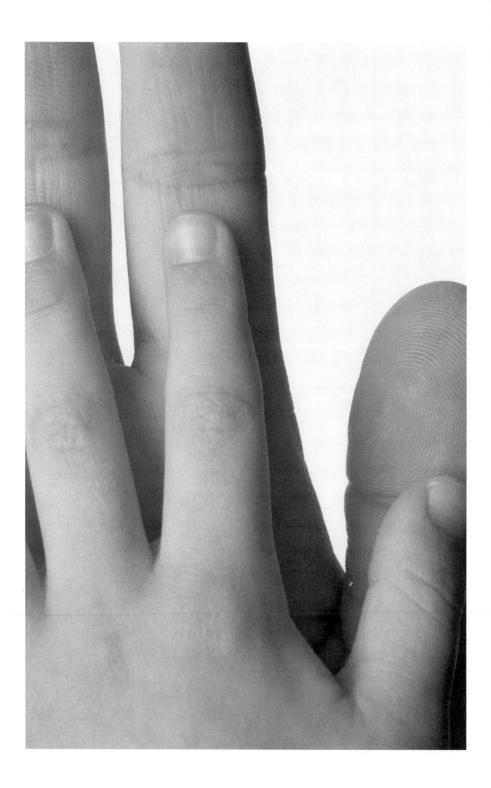

Chapter Four

About Parents

In some situations parents feel they just cannot handle their children's problems, or that they don't know what to do. I don't think this is an unusual situation for parents to find themselves in. But why send the child away if we don't know what to do? We will not spoil a child if we say, "I'm not sure why you're behaving this way, but it sure looks to me like you're upset—so come and sit with me and I will help you find out what you're upset about." The parent, in this case, teaches the child many things. She teaches him that she is not perfect and that answers are not always obvious. She also teaches him that, "If we work together, we can solve this."

Example: "I don't want to go to school today!"
A mother had recently returned to work and so mornings with her two children, ages five and ten, had become challenging. The youngest child, Kathryn, came into her room crying one morning, just as the mother was getting out of bed, declaring that she didn't want to go to school. Explaining to her that

she couldn't stay home with her mother just seemed to make Kathryn more upset, and her behavior escalated to the point where the child was screaming that she "wasn't going to school, and I have a headache and a stomach ache and no one can make me and I hate you."

The mother was frustrated and perplexed about how to handle this, since telling her daughter that she was going to school, even calmly, only seemed to make Kathryn madder. Instead, she took her daughter into bed with her for a cuddle, despite the time constraints of the morning routine, and told Kathryn how much she loved her, and how much she enjoyed having her as a daughter. As she spoke about how she would be thinking about Kathryn at work, her daughter's demeanor changed from being stiff and angry to being gentle and calm. Kathryn still protested that she was not going to school, but now her mother just accepted these statements as expressions of the child's anger at her mother for going to work. After only five minutes, Kathryn jumped out of bed and went to get dressed.

Even though this mother did not know what to do at first, by having a time-in with her daughter, she was able to contain her daughter's feelings and help her prepare for the day. Not allowing Kathryn to have this short time-in with her mother, and forcing her to get ready for school, would have made the whole situation much more difficult for Kathryn. She would not have been able to manage her anger about going to school that morning because she would have experienced another version of the already existing problem—her anger and anxiety associated with her mother's going back to work. Sending her away would have only exacerbated her sense of being alone, her sense that her mother's work was more important than she was, and her sense of no longer belonging to her mother. By taking the time to have a time-in, this mother was able to calm her daughter. The time-in took only five minutes, but had she not spent that small interval with Kathryn, the upset and anger would have taken much longer to cope with and diffuse. Kathryn's anger may well have lasted the whole day and continued to build up daily over time.

Seeing (and refusing to see) ourselves in our children

As parents, it is very important that we do not deny that our children are having problems; we need to see our children realistically. However, we are sometimes afraid to recognize our children's difficulties because they might lead other people— and ourselves—to think that we have not been good enough parents. Despite the fact that we tend to see our children as carrying parts of ourselves within them, when we have problems, we are often unable to acknowledge that our children may have problems as well. Seeing less favorable parts of ourselves in our children makes us uncomfortable with and sometimes angry at ourselves (or guilty). To prevent these feelings, we may try to deny difficulties in our children.

Often the child's problems will escalate to the point where we will not be able to deny them. At such times, again because we don't want to deal with the troubles, or because we don't know how to, we may send the child to her room to "cool off." Perhaps this is better than slapping the child, but in the long run, the rejection may be as damaging as hitting.

Denying that our child is growing up

In the same way that we can be blind to our children's problems, some parents cannot acknowledge that their child is growing up and they do not change the restrictions on the child's behavior. Rather than seeing that bedtimes need to change, or that the child needs to choose his own clothes, or that the child needs privacy, this parent insists that his child still needs the same directions, rules, and routines as before. This is a child who is not "allowed to grow up." The consequences of this kind of care may be that the child does not grow up and remains dependent on his parent for everything—for going to bed, for washing, for dressing, for going out, for having friends, for choosing books, for choosing foods, and many more things. He remains dependent and when he reaches the age of twelve, his parents may balk at such dependency and reverse their directions, saying, "You choose, you do it, it's up to you." When the child then cannot make the choice, or make a decision, and is left with a feeling of confusion, this may cause a sense of worthlessness, a sense that somewhere "I went wrong."

While the child is still young, however, the consequences of parents who cannot let their child grow up may be that, as he develops, he will demand that rules, restrictions, and routines change. He will want his bedtime changed and if it is not changed, then he will get angry. Sometimes this anger will lead to acting out, with the child becoming very belligerent, if not obnoxious. Such children are trying to exert their need for change, but the way they have to go about it only reinforces the parents' view that they're "just not ready for any changes." The situation becomes a vicious cycle, with the parent refusing to change things because their child is not reacting the way they want him to. This parent should talk to his child, choosing one topic, like bedtime, and find out what the child thinks he is ready for.

It is so important to talk and to listen and it is exceptionally important to give a child the time to respond. Too often we answer for the child and don't give him the time to answer. When we do this, we only make the child feel that his answers are unimportant, or that what he thinks is not appropriate, that adults know all the answers—including what the child "should" think and say. The world becomes a very discouraging place for such a child—he feels almost as if there is no room for him.

When parents transfer their anger to their children

Some children are the recipients of their parents' troubles. These children are "scapegoats"; punishing the children's behavior is, in effect, a way for such parents to punish themselves. It is as if the parent feels that "by punishing my child, I'm punishing myself and, if I do that, just maybe, my trouble will stop!" Of course, this never works; one trouble is substituted for another and the child never gets the feeling of being okay. Punishment by rejection, putting the child in isolation, is a technique that some parents use to put their own troubles in isolation, to reject their troubles. It is an interesting way of handling one's own troubles; problems are given to the child and then the child is punished for having them. This strategy will eventually drive the child away and the parent will then say, "I did it for your own good," "You wait and see how you treat your own kids," or "Just be good and we'll all be fine."

Scapegoating is damaging as well as ineffective. If we have difficulty accepting our own vulnerability, our own sense of needing to be nurtured and dependent upon someone, then recognizing these needs in our children will only make us feel helpless and uncertain, if not confused. We have to be aware of the times when we are forcing our children to accept parts of us—those emotions and actions that we find unacceptable in ourselves. I think we have to learn about and accept our own adult feelings so that we do not have to put them on our children. This is difficult. It requires that the parent be the adult in the relationship. It requires objectivity, honesty, and maybe even humility.

If we are able to step back from a difficult situation to do this and to realize that the child continues to need the safety of an adult, then perhaps the best thing to do is to have a time-in for both parent and child. By this I mean that the parent should be able to take some time away from whatever she is doing and sit with the child in a comfortable chair. At this point, the parent might say to the child, "I think we both lost it; we're both upset; and I think it's best if you and I sit for a while and get ourselves 'together.'" I'm not suggesting any great discussions about how both parent and child got into that particular difficulty, rather I'm suggesting a short time-in in which the parent can recognize her own need to be quiet and tolerant—of her own feelings as well as of her child's.

Example: Which one is the poor loser?

To his father, Terry was always a poor loser. Even when he won a game, Terry's father accused him of whining that he should have done better; he didn't actually hear Terry recount the way he played the game. Terry's father could see so many faults in his son, but the worst one was that he saw his son as a poor loser.

Nevertheless, when Terry's first-grade teacher wrote in his report card that "Terry shows excellent sportsmanship qualities, he is fair to other players, follows the rules well, and knows how to handle winning or losing," Terry's father was forced to think about the way he regarded his son. What he discovered was that he hated to lose, that he would walk away from a game if he felt that he might lose, saying that the rules of the game were "unfair" to him, or that other players "ganged up" on him and made him lose. He actually did not realize that he was the poor loser, not his son. He projected his own problem onto his son and then criticized his son for what was his problem. His son had become his "scapegoat container," who protected him from seeing his own faults.

How parents' anger affects their children

There are a lot of things that create anger in parents—from trivial and mundane events, such as a torn stocking, to more serious ones, such as divorce or financial stress. Parenting also evokes anger—anger at kids, or feelings of helplessness and inadequacy that turn into anger. This is natural and normal. Parents get angry when kids won't listen, when routines go awry, when children "spoil" good times with bad behavior. Parenting can be difficult, time consuming, and, often, frustrating. Parents seem to get the most angry when their children are really angry—especially when they are "out-of control" angry, hitting or biting another child. Parents prefer not to have to endure tantrums or shrieking. Ironically, the times when children need their parents the most are often the times when their parents least want to be with them and are most likely to impose a time-out.

What is also ironic is that when children bite or hit other children, the parents react in anger. They worry that their child's misbehavior reflects on them, as if they were personally responsible. In this case, the parents often impose a time-out immediately, to distance themselves from the child's behavior and deny responsibility. They do not want to be seen by others to sanction the behavior. Parents can justify this by characterizing children's rage as an obstacle to the real and important "problem-solving" that parents want to engage in. In one way they are right: anger does block thinking and learning in children as well as in adults. However, these angry feelings present their own opportunity for learning and have to be adequately resolved before children and parents can talk together. Time-out as a strategy for dealing with anger and for helping children to calm down is seriously flawed. Helping children manage their anger by modeling self-control and by accepting their angry feelings are more important and effective responses than using time-out or attempting to immediately resolve the problem that precipitated the outburst.

Time-out is a paradoxical and puzzling response to the urgency of a child's feelings that can only be explained by examining the feelings and needs of the parent. Parents who demand that children "calm down" in an emotional crisis are certain to create confusion, anger, and even despair in their children. Ordering a screaming toddler to sit quietly in a chair for three minutes is like requiring a shy child to perform as a circus clown! It is the parent's need to silence the child that prevails, not the needs of the child to be understood and listened to.

Equally ironic is the parent who sends a furiously upset and angry child for a time-out to calm down. Imagine saying to a sobbing and livid friend who has recently lost a job, "I think you need a time-out. Call me back when you have composed yourself and can talk rationally." A comment such as, "I'm not going to discuss this with you until you have calmed down" in a heated marital debate is sure to provoke the other spouse to greater anger.

Time-out in these situations is a way of avoiding the feelings of helplessness and fear of being a bad parent. When we see "badness" in our children, we want it to go away quickly lest their anger contaminate us and make us "bad," too. After time-out we can all go back to being as nice and rational as we were before the tantrum and thereby avoid our own angry feelings.

Time-in is a way of accepting the helplessness parents and children both feel in the face of out-of-control feelings. It is a way of changing "badness" into "goodness"—theirs, ours, and the anger we create together on days when our needs and moods clash. Angry parents can't parent effectively and their anger can rapidly escalate to yelling and even hitting. Moving quickly to time-in strategies when parents are angry will prevent them from engaging in behaviors that may leave them feeling guilty and remorseful.

Children do not actually cause or create anger in parents and they are not responsible for managing and removing it. Yet, when a child is sent to her room, her parents are really saying, "You made me angry. Go away and stop making me mad." Parental anger is frightening to children. They do not necessarily hear or see parents as they really are because—in that moment—their perception is distorted by their own strong feelings and by the way anger has been handled in the past. When parents take time-in, they can explain their anger and children can see that neither they, nor their parents, have been harmed. A child who is sent away when a parent is angry will be left with a distorted picture of her parent's anger and she will be forced to accept it and take it into herself. This may prevent the child from taking in any goodness the parent tries to offer after the time-out.

Example: The sins of the father...

Gerry was a very angry boy. At nine years of age he tried to hurt younger children by hitting or kicking them. He would destroy things his peers were making and would issue threats like "You're all a bunch of idiots"; "You can't tell me what to do"; "You'll see, I'll beat you up if you don't give me some money." His threats were frightening to other children. Gerry did carry through with some of his threats and it was this expression of his feelings that eventually brought him into play psychotherapy.

Gerry was a physically abused child. Every time he got upset or angry, his parents hit him, telling him to "smarten up" or they would "beat him to a pulp." If he got angry at the playground, whichever parent was with him would hit him, telling him, "Don't you know you can't be angry at the playground?" His parents physically hurt him at the same time that they were saying things like this to him. They never tried to sit with him, contain his feelings, and give him the confidence that someday he would be able to handle his feelings. Instead, after hitting him, they said, "You go to your room to learn your lesson. I'll tell you when to come out." Gerry's angry parents were both essentially saying, "Get out of my sight until you behave the way I say, not the way I do." Needless to say, Gerry became a bully. He copied the behavior that was modeled at home. And he is destined to become abusive, just like his parents, unless someone can teach him about emotions and self-control.

Working with Gerry, his therapist learned that he felt very angry with everyone. He trusted no one and felt that everyone was his enemy and was out to get him. He did not think that anyone could contain his feelings or be a "safe" person for him—and it took several months before Gerry felt that he could tell his therapist how upset he was and why he couldn't trust anyone. As he said, "I'd rather be a loner that a loser." A "loser" was someone who had trusted and been deceived, as he had been by his parents. Gerry had begun to use other children to contain or represent the unacceptable, "loser" part of himself that he then felt compelled to attack.

• • •

The concept that "the sins of the father shall be visited on the son" is terrifying for parents who hope that their children will not repeat their mistakes. Using time-in to teach Gerry emotional self-control and problem solving can help, and could break the chain of abusive behavior in his family.

Example: "Come on, be happy!"

A group of nine-year-olds said that their parents always want them to be happy and if they weren't happy, their parents would say such things as "Get with it and get happy"; "Get out of my sight and don't come back until you have a smile on your face";

"You have no reason to be unhappy, we take care of every-thing—your job is to be happy." These children did not think that they could be happy all the time. In fact, they thought that the idea was crazy and gave example after example of how unhappy their parents were, saying, for example, "They aren't always happy—why should we be?" Eventually this group of children came to the conclusion that their parents did not want to experience the children's unhappiness. Perhaps the parents had enough unhappiness of their own and did not have any energy left over for the children's. The group of children did not know why this kind of situation should exist. All they really knew was that when children are unhappy, they create unhappi-ness for their parents. One young girl wondered out loud whether she should leave home because she was sad, and quickly added that this idea made her even sadder. None of them knew how to deal with the situation, but all the children—all eight of them—realized that it was a problem.

• • •

I wonder whether the parents of these children are judging their own capacities to be good parents by the happiness of their children; judging themselves to be poor parents if their children are unhappy. Perhaps they are overly concerned by what others will think or are overly influenced by books that imply that childhood is a simple and happy time with no troubles or problems. In reality, childhood is not without its troubles and difficulties and, ideally, parents will realize that if their child is unhappy, it is not simply their fault.

There was a time when parents were blamed for all their children's problems and, accordingly, parents have been variously advised by "experts" to love their children more, to be stricter with them, to isolate and punish them, to ignore them; there are probably, many other things that parents have been told that they "should" do to correct the behavior of their children. This kind of advice always put the onus on the parents, as if children do not contribute anything to their own difficulties.

Certainly children cannot raise themselves. Most people would agree that children need loving, caring, nurturing, and guiding parents. Without such parents, we would most likely devolve into chaos and destruction within a generation. Certainly children cannot live without parents; they quite simply need them. But, in addition to what we consider the necessities of life, children also need their parents to be able to deal with the difficult and, at times, unusual feelings that children have—feelings that are not caused by their parents, but arise simply because of the ways children look at things.

Teachers and "difficult" children

Example: Send her away? Or teach her?

A short while ago I was talking with a young mother about her child's difficulties. She expressed concern that he should be able to behave properly at school and not get into trouble in class. Her five-year-old had been refusing to do things in the classroom the way everyone else was doing them. He didn't want to use crayons, he wanted paint. He didn't want the blocks, he wanted to dig in the sand. He didn't want to sit and listen to a story, he wanted to play in the dollhouse. It seemed that whatever the teacher wanted the children to do, he did not want to do. The teacher began to tell him he would have to wait in the hallway until he was ready to do what the other children were doing. In fact, she put him out into the hall every day for a week and then telephoned his mother to let her know that her son was very "difficult." The teacher suggested that perhaps the mother could tell her son to "listen to the teacher or else he'd be spending most of his day out in the hall."

The mother was very upset. She telephoned me for support.

As she talked she remembered that when she was a little girl, her parents had insisted that she go to her room whenever she was a "difficult" child. If she disobeyed or did not obey quickly enough, she was sent to her room She also remembered—with much feeling—that it was then that she began to think that there must be something about her as a person that was very unacceptable. As a child, she remembered thinking, "I'm a bad girl and they don't like me to be with them." She was not able to figure out what it was that was wrong with her. She found herself being sent to her room whenever she did not eat fast enough, when she cried, when she spilled her milk, when she yelled, and when she did not pull up her stockings. As she said, "I never knew why I was being sent away—they just said, 'Go to your room and come out when you can be a good girl.'"

I think that her punishment was quite extreme and agreed with her that she could not have known what was wrong and why, therefore, she had felt that she was unacceptable as a person. What she did learn, however, was to never be angry. She has spent most of her time making sure that she is feeling "un-angry." So when the teacher called her, she was upset. She felt that, once again, she was unacceptable, this time as a mother. There must have been something she was not doing that she should be doing because if she had been doing it, her son's behavior would be fine. When she began to feel angry, she called for a consultation. She was torn between wanting her son to have a good school experience and her own anger at being told she to "do something" so that her son would obey the teacher.

Following our conversation, instead of speaking to her son, the woman suggested to the teacher that when she was ready to announce the next part of the daily routine, the teacher call her son over to her, and holding his hand, make the announcement. As usual, the boy said that he wanted to do something else, but the teacher, accepting the mother's recommendation, suggested that he stay with her. She agreed with him that changing activities seemed difficult, but he had done a fine job at his work, it was now time to move on, and she would help him. He balked at first, but the teacher persisted, and, within a few days, there were no more problems about changing activities.

. . .

I suspect that the boy did not feel that he was "good enough" to do well with the teacher-directed activity and, perhaps, wanted to do an activity that he felt could do well. He needed his teacher to tell him that he had done a good job and was acceptable because, like his mother years before, he felt that there was something unacceptable about him.

Chapter Five

About Families

No parent can ever be perfect for their child. What is possible is to just be good enough for the child, to be the "good enough parents" that Donald Winncott, the British pediatrician and psychoanalyst, spoke of.

No parent can judge when it is best to feed his child so that she will never feel uncomfortable, know whether he smiled just the right way for his child, or whether he gave just the right directions and interactions. It is not possible to do this. We do not ever know exactly how an individual child sees her parent in each child-parent interaction: Does the child feel that the interaction is good enough? If not, then what happens? Because it is never possible to be what a child imagines her parent to be, there will always be some degree of frustration. In fact, I feel that some degree of frustration is a good thing because it spurs development. This "just enough frustration" can help a child look for new ways to do things, new ways to approach her parents, and new solutions to difficult problems. What we can aim for as parents is to be good enough for our child to experience just enough frustration to encourage her to go on to explore new and, perhaps, more effective ways of doing things—including more effective ways of being with her parents.

Helping children identify and verbalize what they are feeling

Children imagine the meaning of what is happening around them based on, or influenced by, their own feelings at that moment. No matter how hard we try to give them information about what is really happening, it is their perception of the situation that matters.

Example: "I want to die!"

One child told his parents that unless he could sit in the front seat of their car, he wanted to die! This statement—not surprisingly—came as a shock to them and they were upset, disturbed, and worried that their six-year-old son was suicidal—a very frightening thought for any parent. Since the boy always had to sit in the rear seat, he began to yell and scream that he wanted to die. When his parents got over the initial shock, his mother sat beside him in the back seat and asked as calmly as she could, "Do you really want to die?" The boy said, "No." She then asked him why he had said that he did and he replied, "When I can't sit in the front seat, I'm very uncomfortable in the back seat." She asked what made him uncomfortable and his answer was surprising: "I'm angry." His mother told him that when he feels angry, he should tell his parents that he is angry and not that he wants to die, and that his anger will not damage them, even if they know how angry he is with them.

• • •

The parents of this child were responding to the way they understood the situation: their son was safer in the back seat than in the front seat. While he told them that he wanted to sit up front, they did not realize the extent of his anger about not being allowed to do so. He could only express this in the most extreme way for him (and for us)—as a wish to die. This, however, did not make sense to his parents and they needed to help him clarify what it was he was feeling. So the first step for a parent is to help the child identify what the problem really is: "Are you angry? Why? Do you feel left out? Is it because you can't see where we are going? Do you think that we don't love you? That we are ignoring you? Does it make you feel car sick?" Once the problem has been identified, the parents can give the child the vocabulary to express the depth or range of the feelings: "Are you furious or just a little irritated? There is a big difference!" (See the "How I Feel" chart on page 38.)

The six-year-old may never like riding in the back seat, but it may help if in the future the parents of this little boy say something like, "We want you to sit beside us, but for your safety and because of the law, children have to sit in the back seat." At least he can get angry at this requirement and not feel rejected by his parents. The child may continue to feel upset and angry, but the basis of the anger he is feeling at that moment will not be what his parents are doing—he can be angry at the safety and legal restrictions rather than at his parents.

Parental control versus controlling parents

Parents are in charge, but being in charge does not mean that parents are in control. Being in control is not the goal; teaching children self-control is the goal. Parents can help their children gain a sense of being in charge of themselves in ways that are appropriate for their age and maturity.

However, for children to be "okay," they need to be in an "okay" family and the members of an "okay" family are in tune with each other's need for time-in. Parents should be able to offer the child a sense of their own control by pointing out what is difficult for the family and/or the situation, and what could make things easier for everyone. In attempting to achieve whatever it is that will make things easier—and it is usually a better attitude towards things—little will be accomplished by sending children away. Children gain a better grasp of themselves and a better understanding of what is needed by being close to a parent whenever they are in trouble or in difficulty.

A child's closeness to her parent carries with it some anticipation. The parent anticipates that, by being close to her, the child will feel better and that, in turn, this support will encourage a more effective identification with parental values and attitudes. Being close to parents, and experiencing their anticipation that this closeness will help the child, is a very powerful motivating force. The child not only feels that she is safe from the possibility that her overly threatening emotions will explode, but that her sense of self-worth (and growing sense of independence) will not be taken away or diminished. In such a relationship, the child has even more "emotional energy" to cope with the stress of her feelings and is more likely to try to do something about the problem.

Time-in to manage relationships

Behavior is shaped by relationships and relationships mean something different to each of us. We all have certain ideas about what other people are like and these ideas usually shape our feelings towards these people. If children imagine that their parents do not want a close relationship with them unless they behave in the "right" way, and that if they do not behave in that way, they will be sent to their rooms, then they have three choices:

1. They can behave in the right way
2. They can become very belligerent and nasty
3. They can withdraw and become excessively quiet

None of these responses are adequate. Children need to know that they can express their feelings and that their parents will help them understand, correct, or modify these feelings. Only then can children manage their feelings. Through time-in, parents and children can discuss how thoughts and ideas about others may be correct or incorrect. They can learn how to change those thoughts and ideas and behave differently, perhaps be more responsive and accepting. In order to do this, children need to be able to think and feel and speak within the confines of a safe and secure relationship. To do this, they need to have time-in with their parents.

Justice must be done…and be perceived to be done

When parents respond to their children and infants in loving and supportive ways, this is a signal—the interaction between what the parent gives and what the baby is able to accept at that time—that becomes lodged in the baby's mind. If the baby is comfortable, if the baby feels well, then the correlation between the outward sign, given by the parent, and the inward sign, provided by the baby's receptivity, comes closer and closer together.

However, there are always some differences between what the baby sees, needs, and understands his parents to be "on the inside," and what his parents actually are "on the outside," or in reality. Parents can never know exactly what their child needs. They do their best to satisfy the child, and yet, sometimes, the child continues to be upset. The child's internal needs and the parent's external satisfaction of those needs may never match perfectly. If I am a tired and cranky child, then, even if my parents are soft-spoken and patient, I still feel them, experience them, and interpret them in the way I am feeling. I am uncomfortable and no matter how much they do, I still feel uncomfortable, so, to me, they are not the giving and nurturing parents I need right now. So I cry and fret and my parents say, "I don't know what to do for you, everything I do is wrong."

It is very important at this point that the parents not give up. If they continue trying to help the ill or overtired child, even though he may not appear to respond at first, he will soon fall asleep. If he has a fever, he will fall asleep feeling that his parents are doing something to help him. For the parents to give up would change the interaction between the real (external) signal offered by the parents and the child's perceived (internal) sign, causing the internal sign to be validated and reinforced by the external. This is not helpful at a time when the child's internal experience is that of a "bad parent" who has not been able to help—"I still have a fever and feel uncomfortable"—and at a time when the child most needs reassurance.

Children make personal interpretations of everything we do. They make sense of their experiences on the basis of how their internal signs—their internal experience of their parents—correspond to their real parents. The saying about justice not only having to be done, but also being perceived to be done has relevancy here. When parents make incorrect assumptions about what a child is feeling, it causes conflicts and problems for the child. In this instance, patient persistence on the part of the parent enables the child's internal sign ("I still feel uncomfortable") to gradually move closer to what the parent actually intends—to be helpful to their distressed child. Although it is often difficult for us in the short term because our internal sign is not perceived accurately by our children, we nevertheless need to help our children learn that they can expect to feel better through experiencing parental patience, tenderness, and more patience. As parents, we need to have our own feelings of frustration, powerlessness, or hopelessness "held" or appreciated by someone else, such as our spouses or our own parents, whenever possible.

Example: The case of the mixed messages

One adult described having always felt that her parents were cold, unloving, and rigid in their relationship with her. She felt that even though they said they were helping her, and from their point of view they were always available to her, this woman felt she had, and still has, an image of her parents as rejecting. She felt that if she was angry their love for her would change, that they would stop loving her. Her internal parental sign was of cold, rejecting parents, yet her parents told her that they were not like that. She has memories of them giving her a certain number of minutes to feel better so that "everyone could go on doing what they were doing." For this woman, the conflict arose out of the discrepancy between what she felt, what her internal signs told her, and what she was told she should be feeling about her parents.

A child's understanding of "bad behavior"

There is always the issue of whether a child actually understands what the adult views as bad behavior that is deserving of punishment. It may be that the child does not understand, or it may be that she does not agree that she has done something wrong. Of course, the child may argue that she was allowed to do the very same thing yesterday: "So why can't I do it today and not be punished?" Sometimes the parent responds with, "Today is a different day!" This does not make very much sense to a child. Why should she be punished for doing something that was acceptable the day before? The parent may then respond that, "I'm tired today and I can't stand that noise." But again, for the child, this still makes no sense—it does not mean that she has turned into a bad person or has done a bad thing. She either becomes angry with her parent or else may feel that she has done something unacceptable without knowing what it was, and feels sad. She cannot predict how to maintain a sense of being a good girl because her behavior is judged by what her parent is feeling rather than by what she is doing.

None of these situations will be tolerable for a child. And on top of this, too often the "bad" behavior is punished by isolating the child "until you behave properly," or by the parent telling the child how "disappointed" he is in her behavior. Very little is more damaging to a child's sense of self-esteem than this. The child does not know how to behave because the cues are not clear or consistent. She may feel not only confused, but time-out will aggravate the situation by communicating that she is not good and is not acceptable.

Example: The good child who was bad

A clear, if sad, example of this occurred in a difficult family circumstance involving a young girl and her mother. This seven-year-old girl had tried to cook. She had woken up early in the morning and wanted to surprise her mother with a cake that she would make "all by myself." She set out to make this cake "just the same way as my mother does." She mixed an unmeasured amount of eggs, water, milk, sugar, salt, flour, and butter into a large mixing bowl. She then cut pieces of bananas into the batter. Next, she turned on the oven. She knew which dial to turn, but, of course, did not realize the temperature she had set for the oven. She placed the mixing bowl with its contents into the oven and left it there until the bowl broke and the batter flowed all over the bottom of the oven and began to seep out onto the kitchen floor.

By now she was becoming upset and frightened and went to tell her mother what happened. Her mother came rushing into the kitchen and began to yell at her daughter, telling her how "impudent" she was "to think she could make a cake," how "unfeeling" she was to have "made such a mess" that her mother had to clean up, and how "bad and nasty she was because she had done such a terrible thing" that "could have sent the house up in smoke and killed them all." The child was sent to her room and told to stay there for the rest of the morning, so that her mother could clean up the "mess" and not hit her daughter. While her daughter sobbed and pleaded, "I wanted to make a cake for you!" she was made to feel like a very bad child who was determined to do bad things. "Nothing like this had happened to the family before," her mother said.

• • •

Perhaps if the woman had told her daughter that they would make a cake together as soon as they (together) cleaned up the cake batter, the child would have not only felt closer to an understanding parent, but would have been able to feel more like the child that her mother loved and so want to be more like mother. The child's self-confidence and self-esteem would have been increased, even though the cake she wanted to make did not work out. However, this was not the case and the girl felt very upset; she felt like someone who did not deserve her mother's love.

A child's sense of responsibility for a parent's distress

It is almost impossible for a child to be all right if his parents are not feeling well emotionally and/or physically. Children derive their strength from us. They are aware that there are times when we are not feeling well or all right. At times like these, the child needs to know that it is not his fault that the adult is unwell. The parent needs to say something like, "I'm not feeling too well today—I have a headache—but I will be well soon. I love you and I know that you had nothing to do with my headache." The child needs reassurance that it was not his fault. I hear parents who say, "Of course, it's not the child's fault; of course, he understands this." My experience, however, does not confirm this. Young children—even six- and seven-year-olds, still consider that their "bad thoughts" or "bad behavior" make their mommy or daddy sick.

If the parents do not give their child reassurance, then the child is apt to feel sick or become unusually quiet or angry. Anger is the child's attempt to fight off the bad feeling that "I am responsible for my daddy's sickness." This may sound paradoxical because the parent may then become even more upset and/or sick if his child is angry, but the child nevertheless persists with this angry behavior, trying to fight off his badness. The child is not trying to get punished; it is not the child's way of saying, "You must hurt me like I hurt you, so punish me." Rather, the child understands this as his best way to get rid of the bad feelings that he is so certain are causing his father's pain. He is sending the anger "out there," so that he won't have those bad thoughts any more.

Another kind of child, the withdrawn child, attempts to pull back to such an extent that he cannot cause his parent pain any longer. Being this withdrawn is a kind of depression in which the child hides and may even refuse to communicate because he believes absolutely that any further action on his part will damage his parent all the more. It is as if this child's conscience is working overtime and he feels very guilty for what he perceives to be his fault, for something that he has done wrong to his parent. Perhaps it is because he has taken "too much" from them, and now his parent is suffering. This child imagines that if he withdraws and presents no further problems, then his parent's illness and/or problem will disappear. In a way, this child thinks that his thoughts and feelings must be so powerful that they can harm or even destroy others; under these circumstances, he feels, it is best to withdraw.

Example: "I think I killed my mom"

One little boy of seven, in play psychotherapy, thought that he had killed his mother because the day before she died, he was so angry with her that he muttered, so that others could hear, "I hope she dies." And, not long after, she did die. This child "knew" that his wish had killed his mother. He had been so angry because she was in hospital and not at home where he needed her to be. He was angry because she was gone. She was not there to help him, to contain his fears, his anxieties, and even his anger. She was not available to him; she went somewhere else because she was sick. But he was also sure that he had made her sick in the first place because he had needed her and his need had just been too great. That's what put her into the hospital. In this child's mind, he had taken so much from her that she became ill. Then, in his withdrawn state, because she was the only one who could help him and she was not there, his anger could no longer be held back. In his anger, he wished her dead and she died.

The child was very remorseful, but few people knew about how he felt. He withdrew and tried to carry on a kind of reparation— his attempt to make up for having caused his mother's death. The first form of reparation was to try to hurt himself. He walked aimlessly into the middle of the traffic and on two occasions was hit by a car. He was not injured seriously, but was hurt enough to feel pain for several days. His father did not acknowledge these "accidents" since the child suffered in silence. But hurting himself did not seem to work, so he decided to try making nice things to leave on the dining-room table, hoping that his dead mother would take them.

• • •

What the boy was doing was offering a kind of sacrifice for what he considered to be his bad deeds. The objects he made were usually drawings and collages that he secretly placed on the table before he went to bed. He didn't want anyone to see him do this and first thing in the morning he would look to see if his sacrifice was still there. Often it was there, but sometimes the table had been cleared and his mother's sacrifice was gone. He was sure it had gone to her. He never looked in the garbage; in fact he refused to have anything to do with garbage. His therapist found this very interesting because if the child had looked in the garbage he might have found some of his sacrifices there. He told his therapist that he never looked, so, in his mind, it was never there. His sacrifices were removed enough times to make him finally think that he had made up for his "badness." Of course, he never forgot about wishing that his mother would die, but in his work in play psychotherapy, he gradually understood how unacceptable his angry feelings were to himself and how much they frightened him. He realized how powerful he thought they were and that he was sure he had killed his mother. He began to understand how much he needed her and could not account for her absence in any way other than to blame himself.

Therapist and child talked about how guilty he felt and how he had been so sure that no one could ever help him deal with his anger that he withdrew. In play psychotherapy he found a time-in—a time when he could feel safe enough to explore his terrible feelings with someone who did not criticize or judge him, and certainly did not punish him. In this time-in he gradually learned to tolerate his own anger and understand why he said and felt what he did. He realized that no one could cause another person's death by wishing for it. "No one is so powerful," he said.

Sometimes children develop various physical illnesses so that they can be in a position where they will not just get the physical attention they need medically, but also be in a position where the adult will protect and nurture them. When a child is ill, the adult keeps the child in bed, sits with him and offers special foods. In these ways, the adult provides time-in for the child. I do not mean that all physical illnesses are caused by scary, bad feelings. However, certainly these scary feelings contribute to actual physical illness and at other times can imitate physical problems. Such problems can be headaches, muscular pains and aches, "sick feelings" and stomach aches. (However, I think it is urgent that every child be medically examined before deciding upon emotions as the cause of the physical problem. Stomach aches are not necessarily always physical in nature, but medical examination is necessary if there are persistent stomach complaints.)

In time-in with a parent, a child gains kindness, sensitivity, empathy, tolerance, tender care, and acceptance. The parent—or another emotionally attuned caregiver—can provide safety for a child at those times of intolerable emotional feelings.

"I can't do anything right!"

Sometimes a child may have the idea that she cannot do anything right, that she is just "no good." Such a child has great difficulty not spoiling everything she lays her hands on. It is as if she "knows" that everything she does will turn out wrong because that's what she has been told so often. But it is not just "things" that go wrong; it is the relationship between this child and her parents that can "never" go right. She feels responsible for that poor relationship because she has not been told that there is something of value in her—something that her parents value and will allow them to keep loving her even when there is a problem. If a child does not think that, as a person, she has any value, or that there is anything she can do about a problem, then she will stop trying to improve the situation. She is so sure that it won't work. As one eight-year-old girl told me, "Anyway, nothing has worked."

Children like this may also try to do nothing; for them, it

seems to be safe: "If you try to do something, then you might do too much. Too many of your feelings will come out and maybe your feelings will get out of control." If that happens, then "You're in for it." It is indeed very frightening for children not to have someone who will help them value themselves by valuing them. It is also very frightening for children—often immobilizing—not to have a person who can help them with their feelings by telling them, "I'll help you with that"—someone who can take over for them when things get overwhelming or frightening. Children need adults to be their safe parents, their boundaries, and their control when they cannot activate these controls themselves. The best way to do this is by being beside the child who is in trouble. "I am here," says the parent. "Fear not."

Even a good child needs time-in

We all know children who at six seem so much more like sixty. They are just so good, never talking back and always doing things just the way that their parents want them to. They go to bed when told, they eat "properly," they do not get into difficulties, and generally they really seem like wondrous children. Well, maybe they are, but my concern is that, in trying to please their parents and be what they imagine that their parents expect of them, they by-pass the ordinary difficulties most children need to experience in growing up. We all have periods of trouble at one time or another. We cannot escape troubles; just growing up is often difficult because our needs are always changing. These children are trying to be too good and too grown up. But in doing this, they miss out on learning how to deal with developmental problems like stress, competition, and frustration. These children do not have the opportunity of working through these problems. They have avoided them by being "too good" at times in their lives when they need to be "difficult."

Example: The perfect boy gets crushed

I know one little boy who, at ten years of age, considered that he was his mother's savior. He was going to protect her from any harm or difficulty and when he couldn't do this he "knew" that he was bad and felt very guilty. He became physically ill. It was not until he understood that he did not have to be perfect for his mother, by being her savior and protecting her from imagined dangers, that he felt well enough not only to challenge both his parents, but to misbehave in mild ways, such as not coming home immediately after school—coming home "ten minutes late," as he said.

. . .

Some children are "too good" because they think their parents will be upset if they have to be "responsible" for them. They want to grow up quickly so they will not be a burden to their parents. They assume that growing up quickly means being good, but it also takes away their confidence in asserting a sense of self, taking risks, and being comfortable in new situations, like school. Certainly parents do not have to use time-out for these overly good children, but they are stumped by their children's lack of self-confidence. When they encourage their children to try new things, they will always try, but they don't know how to cope with the frustrations of not knowing how to do things right the first time. They are used to succeeding quickly and using this to show their parents how good they are. Failing, having to try something several times, means that they are bad. With repeated failure, such children withdraw, trying to reestablish the situation in which they were "good" and could succeed quickly.

Lying

Example: Did she tell a lie?

Most parents feel that lies should be punished. But what happens when a two-year-old girl with a very full and smelly diaper, asked if she made a bowel movement, replies that she didn't, "but Toto [their pet dog] did"? In this instance, the girl's parents told her that she was lying when they cleaned the diaper and showed her the feces. She again answered, "This is Toto's." Her parents called me to ask whether they should punish her for lying and wondered whether they were being negligent if they let this incident go by. I explained to them that two-year-old children do not "lie" in the adult sense. Rather, they are frightened by the questions adults ask because they are not sure whether they have done the right thing. Two-year-olds do not have any real understanding of the word "lie"—it just does not mean anything to them. What does mean something to the child is the emotional tone of the parent. To punish a child for something that she does not understand is, in my way of thinking, abusive.

Instead of telling this little girl that she was wrong, that she was bad or a liar, I suggested that they tell her that the bowel movement was very good and healthy and just the sort that their little girl should make. When the parents tried this, she grinned, and did not reply. However, soon after this incident, she announced that she had made a good, healthy bowel movement! I do not think that this little girl actually understood the terms "good" or "healthy." But her parents had conveyed to her the attitude and feeling that she was a great little girl who was loved and that they were not upset by what she did. With this view of herself, she could then take ownership of herself and her body.

Example: "He bit me!"

The mother of another child, a two-year-old boy, described what happened when she was talking to another friend about plans to have her son in day care in the fall. The situation was calm, the child was playing with his blocks, and the adults were discussing plans. Suddenly the boy came up to his mother and bit her on her breast through her blouse. He had never done this before and his mother was not only shocked, but was also very angry that this had happened—especially when she saw no provocation. After her son had bitten her, she had hit him and sent him away "to learn how to behave properly." She felt that she had done the right thing to ensure it never happened again.

• • •

She did not think that the conversation she was having with her friend had had any effect on the child's behavior, but I pointed out that children do listen to adult conversations and do understand some plans. For example, they understand the statement "my son will be going to day care in the morning." They understand such statements to mean that they will be alone and "mommy will not be with them." Perhaps it is not so much an understanding of each word as it is the emotional impact that such statements make on children. I talked about children's "big ears" and how, even when we do not think children are listening, they are. Children listen to their parents conversations to glean what they can about how to behave, what is going to happen, who is coming to visit, how their parents feel about the visitor, what they expect of their children, and so on.

In this case the child understood he was going away—to some place. The parents had not discussed this either in listening range of their child, or directly with him, showing him where he would be going, for how long, where mommy and daddy would be—all the things that parents should let their children know. Nothing was said to him about day care until he heard it by listening in on the adult conversation. I explained that I thought the child was upset and angry and his reaction was direct. He bit her on the breast—the very breast that had fed him now appeared to be turning away from him and hurting him. So he simply hurt it back.

In talking to the woman about her son, it was clear he was not a malicious child, not an angry boy, but a pleasant, creative, curious, and bright child who enjoyed playing with his parents. The biting was a single incident. To punish him for this was to aggravate the child's sense of being rejected, hurt, and bad. I suggested to the mother that she and her child talk about the incident and that she tell him how surprised she was, but that she understood that he was angry and hurt, and that he, no doubt, felt that he was being sent away. I told her that her tone and expression of feeling were very important. The child would need to gain a sense of being wanted and loved—not just by the words, but also by the feelings they expressed. This biting behavior has not reoccurred and this mother has been able to give her son back the sense of being wanted that he had always felt before, and the reassurance that day care was simply another step in growing up, not a rejection.

Fathers and time-in

Fathers are very important in their infants' and babies' lives. But the way I see it, the father's first role is as a support to his wife—someone who tries to make sure that the experience of mother and baby are as free from tension, turmoil, and frustration as possible. He helps her to maintain the first relationship with the baby, supports her in doing this, takes direction from her in helping her and the baby, and "moves in" when she needs and asks for help. He does not just "take over"; he does not try to prove he is a better parent than she is. There is no competition for parenting. Gradually, he takes on more and more of a role in fathering, but usually this is still under the mother's direction. In other words, he does not usurp her role, he complements it. He accepts her work with the baby without experiencing jealousy. This is not easy for most fathers to do, but it is something I know fathers can learn.

Example: The boy who thrived

There are times in a family when the father does take over—when he is the primary caregiver. Then the mother is the supportive person. In a family I know, where the father was the primary caregiver for the first four years of their son's life, I noticed that the child related very well to both mother and father. He got along very well with his peers, he was secure in his relationship to his parents, he entered day care at three years of age, and was not disturbed by the separation experience. On the second day, he decided that he did not want to go to the day care and his father had no difficulty allowing his son to stay home with him. It seemed that this boy was doing well all around. In his very early experiences, his father took on the role of containing his anxieties, of helping him develop first a oneness with his father and then a gradual separation from him. There was the usual swinging back and forth from being separate to being attached, but they encountered no unusual difficulties. When the boy was ill, he went to his father, when he wanted to go to sleep, he chose his father at first, but when he was two years old, he asked for "anybody to put me to sleep." He was weaned from the breast within the first month. His mother returned to work after three months of staying at home with her son and husband. Instead of being the supported one, the father was supported as soon as the mother felt well enough to go back to her job; the boy thrived in this arrangement.

• • •

I think that while there is an ongoing relationship with the mother—that probably starts when she realizes she is pregnant, and is deepened when she feels the baby move inside her—the relationship's strength and love can be transferred to the father when the parents have discussed their plans and have realized what roles they are to both play in rearing their infant. While the father can only imagine the birth process and the breastfeeding relationship, he can nevertheless accept that the mother will start the relationship with the newborn; he will carry on that strong relationship with her help and, at first, under her direction. Soon he has the primary relationship and the mother then supports this by nurturing both of them. In the family I know, this worked because neither the mother nor the father felt threatened or jealous of each other. Unfortunately, this is not the case in most families, where this strong support is lacking. In these families, the relationship with the spouse is not as containing or filled with the comfort that is so often needed.

Chapter Six

Growing up and Growing Apart

Separation is a very important milestone in every child's development and the way in which this is handled is crucial for future healthy growth. If we demand separation at too early an age, we set the stage for problems—for example, the exacerbation of sleeping problems. Sending the child away from her parent because the child is having a problem will have major repercussions on the way in which the child is able to separate from the parent in the future.

Example: "Why isn't she sleeping through the night?"

One young baby of nine months had been weaned at six months because her mother had to return to work and a sleeping pattern that had not been a problem became a very serious problem. In the first few months, the baby woke up a few times every night and was nursed back to sleep. Then at six months, she was weaned by replacing the nightly nursing with bottle feedings. The baby responded by refusing to go to bed, howling when she was placed in her crib, refusing to be fed or comforted and finally falling asleep only out of exhaustion. When her mother called me, she told me that the baby was accepting a bottle during the daytime while her mother was at work. The nights were the problem—no one was getting enough sleep. I suggested that they put the baby in their bed, lie beside her, and sing to her. If she cried, the parents were to continue singing softly to her and offer her warm cuddles and the opportunity to suck on a bottle. The parents were afraid that they would fall asleep in their bed with the baby and harm her. I gently pointed out that, while this could happen, I suspected it was their anger at their daughter that was at the root of this worry. I suggested that they could make a bed roll and offer her a safe spot, a nest, in the bed—the baby couldn't roll out and the parents would meet some resistance should they roll too close to her.

The parents decided to follow these recommendations, but only one of them would fall asleep; the other would remain awake. The mother chose to lie down with the baby and follow the recommendations. Within a week the baby's sleep seemed normal enough for the mother to put her back into her own crib. This didn't work, however, and she brought the baby back to her own bed. The parents were afraid that they would spoil their daughter if they continued to allow her to sleep with them in their bed. They did not seem to understand that as their daughter gained a sense of comfort and satisfaction, she would have enough confidence in her own competency to be able to try sleeping alone in her own crib.

• • •

This thinking goes against many popular theories and popular wisdom. Let me explain. It is only as a result of our self-confidence that we are able to accomplish most things. We are not being spoiled, but what we are doing is gaining a sense of being able to deal with our own feelings. It is our relationship with our parents that enables us to do this. The better the relationship, the more secure it is, the more effective will the baby be at meeting her own needs, because the well-attached baby knows that she can always come back to the parent for comfort if she needs it. This attachment is an extremely powerful aspect of the baby's relationship to the parent—and it should be the kind of attachment that actually helps the baby want a sense of independence. Only "securely attached" babies will try to become effectively independent; it is because of their sense of security within the relationship to their parents that they are able to explore separation. So rather than spoiling a baby by helping her fall asleep, we actually enhance the baby's competence at being able to fall asleep alone.

The little girl in the example above took three weeks to "settle" her sleep problem, a problem that had continued for at least three months. I think that it was only after the parents began to realize how angry they were at being so tired that they were able to provide the safety and boundaries that allowed their baby feel a secure "reattachment" to the mother. Within this reattachment, the baby was able to develop her own sense of competence to the point where sleeping was no longer a problem.

Example: "It's like you're in my pocket."

Another little girl, a three-year-old, was able to describe in very clear and effective language what I have been trying to say. As her mother reported, "My three-year-old came back to me a week after I'd told her that she didn't have to copy everything her friend says because she has her own special voice inside her. She must have mulled over this one. On reflection she said, 'You know, Mommy, I don't only have Amy Smith [her friend] inside me. I have a part of you and daddy inside me, too—it's like you're in my pocket all the time, so I can keep you safe, but it's really inside me and it keeps me safe, too.'"

• • •

This securely attached little girl feels she has the kind of relationship with her parents that helps her to feel safely independent.

Weaning and a sense of loss (in the mother)

Mothers also realize their own sense of disappointment at weaning their babies, even if they had planned it. I think that this sense of disappointment is related to their anger at having to give up something that they find pleasing and enjoy watching their babies enjoy. For many mothers, there is a deep sense of loss. I think that we respond to loss with anger—anger that arises from a sense of frustration. The baby is frustrated because there is a change in the way he is comforted and the mother is frustrated by losing her sense of herself as a nurturing mother. She will have to change the way in which she nurtures her baby. We usually do this quite automatically, as, for example, when we say to ourselves or out loud, "My baby is old enough now to drink from a bottle." Or, "He is ready to try new foods." Or, "I will be going back to work in a few months and I have to consider weaning him from the breast."

Statements such as these indicate the ways in which we suggest to ourselves that our anger or irritation is not something real. "It's because the baby is growing up." We want our babies to remain babies and, at the same time, we want them to grow and mature! We may acknowledge the paradox, but not the extent to which it shields us from our own anger. Some mothers, despite their attempts to see "weaning as a good thing," nevertheless express periods of sadness and crying. I think that this is an outward expression of some unacknowledged feeling—like anger. A mother might rightly say, "I'm not angry with my baby," but she may say instead, "The baby is angry at losing the breast." But the mother also has to give up something important to her—the comfort and care that the nursing provides; comfort for her and care for her baby. To cope with this loss, she will have to find another way to provide comfort and care to her developing child. She will have to reconcile herself to her child's development and adapt her mothering to this changing baby. The father, as well, will have to make a similar adjustment in his fathering role, but his relationship with his baby at this stage is not usually as "primal" as that of the mother.

Weaning and a sense of loss (in the baby)

In the same way that parents experience this loss, so does their baby. Depending on the way that this loss is handled, few problems need arise. If the parents realize that a sense of loss creates irritation and allow for these feelings to be expressed in their baby's behavior, then the difficulty will soon be overcome and the family will have moved to another "level of maturity." If they do not give themselves and the baby time to experience these changing feelings, then problems may persist for long periods of time and only become more intense as the baby continues to grow; the foundation for most emotional difficulties is laid very early in life. Unless these issues are dealt with, the responses will become more exaggerated. So a baby who has sleeping problems after weaning may also become the toddler for whom toileting is a struggle. Having to give up the breast or bottle was hard and now the child is asked to give up the "freedom" of toileting in a diaper and is expected to toilet in special places at special times. This is another loss, even though it is not thought of in the same way as the loss of the breast or bottle. Since the first loss was not resolved, the second one may meet with resistance as well.

Moving

Example: "We don't want to move!"

A family I knew was moving and their three children were having a "fit." The children were angry, balking, and irritable, and they were complaining that all their friends were at the old place and they "didn't know anybody at the new place." The three of them, ranging in age from six to ten, were adamant about not moving and would raise a daily litany of reasons why. In speaking to the parents about the forthcoming move, I talked about separation and loss and the resultant anger. They pointed out that the children had no choice in the matter; they just had to move and "that's that!" As we discussed this more fully, I tried to help them realize that their children felt as if they were losing part of themselves, that they felt as if "a part of them would stay in the old house and they'd never be able to get it back again." The parents could understand this, but argued that although, for example, they would miss the conveniences that they had built into this house, they were going to give them up to get even more conveniences. I pointed out that the children couldn't see it that way; nonetheless, there might be some things they could do as a family to help the children cope with this loss and separation. I suggested that each member of the family take photographs of the house and surroundings "their way" and that they create an album of their "old house." In addition, each member of the family could choose some perennial flowers and, if possible, a tree, and some rocks from their old garden to transplant in the new one. While the parents were skeptical about this, they said that they would "talk it up" that evening. The children's response was immediate. They liked the idea and set out to decide what they were going to photograph and what part of the garden they would bring to their new house.

· · ·

I think this recommendation worked for this family. Even though the children were angry about the move, they nevertheless were prepared to try to deal with their loss as long as the parents were able to offer them some strategies to deal with the pain of separation. If the children or adults had not been prepared to "deal with" the separation, then more than simple recommendations about what to do would have been required. Most vital would be a few sessions with the whole family, in which we could talk about loss and separation so that past separations and unresolved loss and anger could be touched on. This would give all the people involved a greater opportunity to accept that there are some very positive things that can be done to alleviate anger.

Introducing loss gradually

Whenever we can, I think it is important to introduce loss gradually. In this context, I don't only mean weaning, but also toilet training, going to school, moving house, moving to another school, and so on. It is important that not only adults have a chance to think about change—and the impending loss of something that is known and recognized; it is equally important that children be given time to get to know how they feel about it.

Many children will not be able to deal with subsequent feelings when loss and change are suddenly imposed them. They will either cut off their feelings because there is too much anxiety for them to cope with, or they will become "problem children" and begin to balk at whatever they are told to do. If we are not given the opportunity to try to settle such feelings, then we will almost certainly react to other situations and events the way we reacted to the original change and loss.

As adults, we try to react appropriately to loss—and most of the time we do. It is only when there is some really important loss that we discover how we really feel and begin to recognize how we felt about some loss that happened a long time ago when we were children. I'm talking about the death of a loved one, where that loss brings on a flood of feelings: sadness, withdrawal, and anger. We cry at the loss of a dear friend and, at the same time, recall the pain we experienced at the death of a parent. Anger at the loss of a loved parent or friend may be expressed when we say, "Why did that have to happen? Why did it happen now, just when things were going so well for her? Why now, when she had just moved into her wonderful new apartment." Our anger at the loss is mixed in with our bewilderment. Children react to most situations in this way: "Why do I have to leave the game? Why can't I stay longer? Why do I have to leave just when I'm having fun?" I don't mean to imply that leaving a game is the same as experiencing the death of a loved one, but rather that our own emotions are often much stronger than we recognize and children's emotions are equally strong, even though they are sometimes very hard to understand.

We cannot expect children to react the way we do when they move to a new house. We often don't acknowledge their feelings and the strength of their emotions. Children do feel these changes acutely and they often respond in ways that we just don't like. We need to allow children to feel upset and angry at times of change and separation and we need to acknowledge why they feel the way they do. We shouldn't say, "You don't have to feel like that, you're a big boy now." Rather, we need to let them know that "We all have these upset feelings, but we will all be together and we can talk about the nice things we did at the old house." Parents need to contain their children's anxieties, not dismiss them as nonsense or hope they will just diminish with time.

Starting day care

Starting day care is a very difficult experience for most children. Some parents expect a child to just accept the decision that he will go to day care in a way that is far beyond his level of maturity. It's impossible for a child not to respond to changes in his life, and, while the change is not actually part of his development, it is an event that he will have to take into his overall being. In other words, he is going to have to integrate the change. To do so, the child will let other developed behavior slip until he has understood and begun to absorb the idea of being separated from his parent, even if it is only for a morning or an afternoon.

Parents get upset and even angry when a child does not seem to accept new events such as day care easily and without turmoil. They feel that their parenting skills have been poor and that someone will think they are not good enough parents—often their own parents. Some parents have actually punished their child with time-out in order to subdue any reaction. As a punishment technique, this is senseless because it is the very thing that the child is having trouble with—separating from his home and family. With time-out, the child may learn to control his feelings, but the cost will be very high. It will be difficult for him to judge how others are feeling towards him. He will not be able to judge what his parents' expectations are for him because he will have turned away from others. His parents have hurt him for the very feelings that would allow him to understand and be sensitive to others. He will have to "close-down" these emotions because they lead to feeling hurt and rejected. Of course, this does not mean that he will be an "emotionally disturbed" child. What it may mean, however, is that an important area of development will be limited—the ability to recognize how people feel toward him. He believes that he will have to limit his need to depend on adults because they do not understand that he needs them more at some times than at others.

Social growth and development does not occur all at once. Rather, social growth includes the capacity to be dependent on safe and understanding parents, so that one can predict that they will be there when needed. That allows children to accept the risk of being alone because they know they can count on their parents if and when they need them. Social growth includes this sense of independence and a quality of aggressiveness. The ability to "strike out on your own" takes a certain degree of aggression—positive aggression or "feistiness" —the kind of cockiness you see in babies when they know they have mastered some action. Children will not strike out on their own if they are concerned that their expression of aggression will either not be accepted or will be punished, that is, if they are made to feel that they did "too much" on their own, that they went "too far." Parents of such children often have difficulty helping their children achieve the very independence they are asking for and these children become very rule-bound, always looking to their parents to make sure that they are doing things the way their parents want them to.

Leaving Home

Example: Camp as punishment?

One six-year-old boy, describing his initial camping experience the year before, when he was five years old, said that he thought that the separation from his family was terrible. He was sure that everything would go on without him in his absence from home and that he would never be able to catch up to what was going on. He was, in his words, "missing everything" and if he stayed away, there would be no place for him on his return. He didn't think that his parents would not want him to come home, but that they would have had all sorts of experiences that he had not been part of. To him, this meant that he was no longer going to be a part of the family.

This boy's feelings were so strong that he tried to run away from the camp and, when he was brought back, he complained of being ill. He was put in the infirmary and left on his own, which only increased his concerns about being part of a family. He was so sure that he would be forgotten and then, in his six-year-old mind, if he was forgotten by his parents, he would cease to exist.

This young child was not prepared to be separated from his family. His sense of his own position in the family must have been very vague already, leading him to feel as if he did not belong unless he was there all the time. Of course, what he was trying to tell the camp counselors by running away and becoming ill was that he was not prepared to be separated from his family. His feelings of being attached to his parents was in jeopardy and he was trying his best to get home so that he could continue to feel like a person.

. . .

Separation from parents is always difficult. Some children are more prepared to separate from their parents than others. I think we understand a bit more about how different kinds of separation affect children. We are aware that some children have difficulty with separation when they leave their homes to go to school. But some children also have difficulty when they change schools, even though they might be with the same teacher or children they had been with for the past several months.

Example: When changing schools causes anger, confusion, and loss

A four-year-old girl had moved from one school building to another. Although she had visited the new school on a few occasions, she reacted to being in her new classroom by refusing to come out of the cloakroom. She stayed there, holding onto her coat for about an hour, refusing to either sit or move. Her teacher, whom she knew, visited her several times, but the child simply refused to come into the classroom. When she finally came in, holding onto her coat, she sat herself right in front of the teacher, looking at her intently. Whenever the teacher had to move, the child looked back at the cloakroom, but followed the teacher, trying to remain as close as possible to her.

Another four-year-old boy told his parents that he did not

want to go to the "new school" because, he insisted, none of the children he knew would be there. "The teacher won't be there!" he exclaimed. His parents brought him to the class, but the ride to school and entering the classroom was a tearful experience for the child. When he finally came into the classroom, he told his teacher that she had to read the same story that she had read to the class for most of the past week, "A Difficult Day." He remained close to her and insisted that all he could do was play in the sand, saying, "I don't want to play with anybody." He seemed jumpy and quite unable to settle, a characteristic that was unlike his usual behavior.

Still another young boy announced to "the whole school" that his new classroom was not as nice as his old one. The teacher told him that she thought that the new classroom was "much brighter" than the old one—to which he responded, "It's not as bright as my old classroom." His old classroom had been in a basement.

· · ·

Some children and their parents made a map of the new route that they had to take to get to the new school. They surveyed the area, labeled the streets, and marked their house, the new school, and some significant buildings on route to the new school. The children made sure that they looked at their map several days before the move, and used the map to "help" their parents find the right streets and the "right" new school. A young boy got very excited when he discovered that the new school was really at the "end of the street—just where it is supposed to be."

When children move from one school to another as a group, and when they move from one home to another, there is a sense of loss and sadness. I think the feeling of loss is a kind of re-creation of their original loss of mother during their weaning period. When children have to give up something that gives them comfort and a feeling of satisfaction, anger is associated with the loss. The anger may be seen and felt by the mother in the form of biting the nipple if they are breast fed, or refusing to suck—a refusal to do the very thing that they want to do. Some mothers experience this upset as a feeling that arises out of changes that their baby is going through—"He's different now, maybe he's just growing up" or "He has some trouble falling asleep now." They are not able to recognize that the "upset" feeling is anger and is associated with their baby's sense of loss.

Grief and mourning

When a child's parent or an important relative dies, grief and mourning become part of that child's life. It is so important at these times to be able to tolerate the child's feelings along with the intense feelings the adults have. It is important to help the child express these feelings and not "bury" them. It is cruel to leave a child alone at such a time—abusive, in fact. It is urgent that a child in mourning be with someone who can tolerate her pain and loss. Time-in is vital and could be said to be every child's right.

Example: "How should I act?"

Maya, a five-year-old, responded to the announcement that her grandfather had died with "Let's go out and have some ice cream." Her parents were shocked that she would say this when they knew how close she was to her grandfather. They became very angry with her and lectured her about "feelings" when someone dies. Her quiet response to them after they finished their lecture was, "I was afraid that if I cried, you would get even more upset."

Example: "Auntie died, are you going to die, too?"

Romi, an eight-year-old, told his parents that he didn't care that his aunt had died. "She wasn't very nice and she smelled." His parents were very upset and sent him to his room "to learn not to say such bad things." Romi went to his room and broke all his "constructions"—his airplane models. When his father asked why he did this, Romi replied, "I needed to punish myself because I am very bad."

. . .

If the parents had recognized that these children needed to have "safe" time-in with them and understood the children's words as their reactions to intense feelings, then both the children and their parents might have had an easier time dealing with the death of a loved one. Parents, even when they are distressed by the death of someone close to them, need to know how important it is that they remain close to their children. When a relative dies, children imagine that their own parents may die; they need to be reassured that their parents are well and are able to handle not only their own feelings, but also those of their children. Children will deny the death of a relative, will become angry, or will behave as if the death doesn't matter to them, when actually they are worried about their own parents' health. Reassuring them and making them feel safe will enable them to express their emotions of grief and mourning.

Dealing with serious illness and crises

Example: "Is Mommy okay?"

A young woman with two children was rushed to the emergency room and did not have any time to prepare her children, aged two and six, for her departure. The children were not able to visit her until the next day. Although their father tried to comfort them, they remained anxious and distraught about being separated from their mother.

As soon as she was feeling better and on the mend—before the children were to arrive—the mother expressed concern about being able to accept the children's anxieties and allow them to talk about their feelings of being separated from her and "left alone" for the night. Sometimes, when children are separated from a parent, they think that the parent is angry with them. Or they are angry with the parents. I suggested that she ask her husband to bring crayons and paper with him when he brought the children and, in order to help them express their feelings, she encourage them to make drawings of the hospital room. This would give their mother the opportunity to help the children ask questions about what they were drawing. During this process she could encourage them to talk about their feelings and concerns. I felt it was important for the children to realize not only that they had nothing to do with her emergency hospital admission, but also that she was not "sick." Rather, she would help them see that she had a problem and needed the hospital to help her, that the hospital was helping her, and she was getting stronger every minute. Soon she would be strong enough and well enough to leave the hospital.

When the children first arrived and started drawing, they concentrated on distant things, such as the door and wall, only gradually moving in on the object that was most important to them—their mother in the bed. The questions about what, why, when, and how long then came quickly and the drawings and scribbling continued, with their activity serving as a vehicle for conversation. Children, and adults as well, are able to talk more when they are doing something. Perhaps the activity defuses the emotion. Or perhaps, by drawing, they are able to make aspects of a difficult, complex, and abstract world concrete. They are able to relate to something that might otherwise be too intricate and intense for them. When they draw it, they select and concentrate on what is important to them, while leaving out all those other bits and pieces that can further complicate their feelings.

The visit went well and the children were able to leave with the promise of many telephone calls before the next visit. They wanted to know why Mommy would not be home to give them lunch or tuck them into bed at night. Their mother told them that she would be thinking of them at lunch and at bedtime, and that they should phone her before lunch and bedtime and tell her what they were doing. She also showed them on a calendar that there were two days before she would be home, telling them again how much stronger she was feeling and how good it was to see them. Children have a difficult time holding onto good feelings inside themselves when they are frustrated and upset; they need to be reminded of these small nurturing signals to make sure that their (internal) "good mommy" was not in danger of becoming a "bad mommy." Their mother took the opportunity to do just that when she asked them to telephone her before important daily events, letting them tell her what they were about to do.

• • •

I think it is essential in a situation like this that the parent not "whine" about, for example, how much she misses the children, or about how much better it is at home. All this does is reinforce the idea that the children are either not to enjoy themselves while their parent is in hospital, or that the parent, in some fantastic way, is blaming the children for the fact that she is in hospital. Neither of these scenarios is good for the children. Rather, the parent should be able to let the children talk about what they want to talk about, to encourage their questions, and to never make children feel that they are responsible for the sickness.

Example: What the children needed from Daddy

While their mother was in hospital, the children were becoming irritable, almost frenetic, not able to settle to anything and constantly under foot. The father had a lot on his plate. He had to juggle his work, the house, and his wife's needs, to say nothing of the needs and demands and worries of the children. His own anxieties interfered with his parenting in that he kept trying to get the children to be calm, not to worry, saying, "Mommy is fine, you'll see her soon." None of this was much help. When the children continued to be irritable, his first reaction was to send them to their rooms, where they would "at least be out of sight." Fortunately, when he spoke to his wife, they decided together that the children's upset was due to their concern about not seeing their mother and that sending them to their rooms would only suggest to them that they were a nuisance and that their worries were not real. In no way could these young children cope with the worries they were having, adjust to these concerns, nor adapt to this event by themselves. They needed time-in. They needed their father's patience and understanding and that is just what he next gave them—time-in with him to help calm them and prepare them for their first visit to the hospital.

• • •

A time-out during a crisis makes a child believe that what "used to work okay before" is not working and it has made her "bad enough to be sent away." The child experiences considerable confusion during a crisis. She also experiences very concretely the upset caused by a parent not being there as a pain, literally a physical pain, accompanied by a mounting sense of panic. To imply to the child that she can cope with the confusion, the sense of panic, and the physical pain is too much for most—if not all—children. As adults, we don't want to be alone when we're terribly upset; why should children? Perhaps it is our own feelings of impotence, of not knowing how to help our children, that forces us to send them away at just the times when they need us most and must be able to count on our strength to help them through a crisis.

Understanding patterns of age-appropriate development

When we think about the development of a young child, we need to consider the way that a child actually progresses. Progress is not made all at once, nor is it made in all areas of development at the same time. This might almost be considered a well-known truism except for the fact that I have talked to so many parents who are concerned when the "control" their child was showing a week ago suddenly seems to be lost.

Example: Baby steps backwards

An eleven-month-old boy I know had been developing very well, even starting to do the kind of walking that is often referred to as "cruising"—holding onto a coffee table with one hand and maneuvering his way around and around the table. His parents praised him and he responded to their loving reaction to his magnificent feats of walking. He began to take his hands off the coffee table and to stand there as if suspended in space. Then, ever so casually and under control, he dropped down to the floor. He had mastered the difficult physical acts of balancing alone, and by not falling, of sitting down. He was so happy—he burst out with smiles, chuckles, and loud vocalizations.

His parents expected that he would soon move on to walking and he did within about a week. Having accomplished this major task, he then concentrated on sounds, repeating very special vocalizations. His walking didn't stop as he increased his vocal activity, but as his parents described, "He won't let go of the coffee table, he won't take any more steps by himself, and, in fact, he seems to want to be held much more—suddenly he's a much younger baby." They were upset and, of more concern, disappointed in their baby's development; they even considered that there might be something wrong with him. When they described their son's activities, they voiced these anxieties, although they focused on the idea that maybe they were not stimulating him enough—maybe it was their fault.

• • •

I pointed out that what was happening was certainly not their fault, that most children follow a pattern of development in which they move ahead in one area— concentrating on that area of development—and nothing else seems to matter. The mother said, "You mean that's why he was not as interested in food and eating as he had been before he went on his walking spree?" She recalled that after he began to look confident about his walking, "food and eating were not as big a thing as before." Now that the baby is concentrating on talking and communicating, his walking has taken a back seat. In fact, it is less effective than it was just a week ago. What usually happens is that within another week or so, he will be able to vocalize the way he wants to, and then his walking abilities will suddenly jump forward again. He will walk just as well as—and probably better than—he did just before he lost interest in getting around by himself. While he was dealing with new and difficult speech-related tasks, not only did his walking look "worse," but he was also "off his food" and bedtimes were difficult. He did not want to be by himself. While he was, at least temporarily, letting go of advances he had already made in favor of his newly evolving speech, he needed more time-in with his parents.

Parents often become very upset by what seems to be a backward step in development and do not support their child when the child needs their closeness. They insist that the child walk because he walked before, that he eat because he is such a good eater, and that he also go to bed in the same way that he did before these changes in development occurred.

Eating: The battle for control

I have often wondered about parents who tell their children not to stuff their mouths or who criticize them when they save some small piece of food "until the last." When some children stuff their mouths—usually to the despair of their parents— the children get smiles on their faces and look so contented and

117

satisfied. I relate this satisfaction of a full mouth to the experience of warmth and affection from their mothers. I think that most of us have experienced this: When your mouth is full of good food, it is like having a good-enough mother fill you up. And children are not the only ones who like to leave the very best piece to the last, to save the best morsel to relish at the end. I see adults doing the same thing, keeping themselves tantalized until the very end of the dish.

When parents put too much food on a child's plate and the child becomes picky and fussy, refusing to eat, saying she has too much on her plate, this is, I think, a case of "crowding." Children, as well as adults, have difficulty with feeling crowded and try and organize their surroundings so they have some space for them- selves. Putting too much food on a plate is a form of crowding the child and the child's reaction is to become irritable. Put less food on the dish, allow a space between different foods, and rely on children's feelings of hunger and satisfaction to let them know when to ask for more.

Example: Controlling versus teaching self-control

A pair of two-year-old boys were allowed to eat whenever they wanted to. They were encouraged to ask for food when they felt hungry and, even though they had several snacks each day, they participated in family mealtimes. The mothers of the two boys were criticized and told that their children would not only be picky eaters, but that they were "spoiling" their children. With some support, both mothers continued to follow their own advice, although they did have a hard time dealing with all the criticism they were getting—even from their own families!

Both children are now five years old and both are excellent eaters. There are no feeding hassles and meals are usually a pleas- urable time. The mothers are not worried that their children are not eating enough and both children are curious enough to taste all sorts of foods. There were some difficulties in the beginning—for example, one of the children sometimes said that he did not want to sit at the table with his parents. On those occasions, he was given the alternative of sitting at the kitchen counter and would begin to eat his food there, only to return quickly to the table for fear that he might miss some discussion going on between his parents.

• • •

Control over food seems to represent control over feelings and, for children, this means that the very concrete control over food becomes representative of control over themselves. Children can do some things independently and are willing to try; they are also capable of asking for help when they see they that they need it. When the parent insists on maintaining control over food, the parent is taking control over behavior. As one father said, "When I control the food, I can have some peace." It is too bad this father does not realize that what may seem like control right now will become a battle in a few months or years over who is in charge, as the child establishes her independence and her need to be in charge of herself. The gain in control this father is getting right now may be offset by future estrangement from his child.

Example: Food, spoiling, and satisfaction

Just such a problem arose with a two-and-a-half-year-old girl. When the parents managed the food and told her that she could not eat between meals because she'd lose her appetite, she began to smear her feces. The parents were very upset by this change in their daughter from a neat, clean little girl to a smearing, messy child almost overnight. The problems usually occurred at night. She would have a bowel movement, put her hand into her diaper, and smear the feces all over her crib, herself, the wall—over whatever she could touch. When the parents asked for help, I suggested that they make food and eating less restrictive and that food be given freely whenever the child asked for it. The parents were very worried about the smearing, but this seemed to be overridden by another concern when they asked, "Won't we spoil her if we give in to her demands?" I told them that food and satisfaction would not spoil her, but it was interesting that, while smearing was definitely upsetting to them, it appeared to take second place to spoiling!

As we talked about food, spoiling, and satisfaction, I also recommended that the parents give their daughter puddings to eat—puddings that she could freely smear over her high chair and even over herself if she wanted to, and that they not put her out of sight when she did this. I also suggested that they allow her to taste the smeared puddings. The parents wondered if this wouldn't encourage her to taste her feces, but I pointed out that we didn't really know that she wasn't already doing this because she did have feces on her face. With mixed feelings of disgust, annoyance, and despair, they agreed to allow her to use the puddings in this way if she wanted to. She is now three years old and there are no smearing problems, either with the feces or the puddings; the feces smearing stopped within a couple of weeks.

* * *

A four-year-old boy best summed up the issue of food, feeding, mother and father, control and freedom in this conversation with his mother:

Mother: Do you have a mommy inside of you?
Teddy: Yes.
Mother: Is it a good mommy or a bad mommy?
Teddy: A good mommy.
Mother: What does she do?
Teddy: She gives me her nipple to suck whenever I need it.

(And at this point he slipped his thumb in his mouth and began to suck.)

Play and the need for time-in at a distance

Sometimes parents are concerned about how often or how much they should play with their baby or young child. They may recognize that the child does not need a parent to play with her, but does need enough interaction to keep the play from getting stale. While mother and baby are quiet, with the baby playing and the mother watching, the baby will quickly become engrossed in play. After a few minutes, the mother's comment on the play enables the baby to become more involved and more engaged in the play. The theme of the play does not change, no new toy is introduced into the play, and the mother has not moved from her spot. She simply talks to her baby, periodically commenting on the play.

Parents often become "too involved" in their baby's play. They bring in too much, make inappropriate suggestions, take over the play, and try to teach the baby how to do something when she is engrossed in another aspect of the play or is not yet ready for new suggestions. In many ways, parents may overstimulate their baby or stimulate her inappropriately. Babies need their parents to watch what is going on, to let the activity develop, and then comment on what has been going on—not on what is going to happen. Comments do not require either new materials to be brought in, or a change in the activity theme. I find that many parents are disappointed in their child's play, thinking that it is "too low-level" or that the play needs "a change of direction." Usually, neither is effective. If the play is changed, the child will leave the activity altogether. She may just throw the toy away and start to cry or sit there not doing anything.

None of these interventions will help the child develop adequate play behavior. Parents who get angry with their children for not following their directions or instructions might consider that their recommendations are too far in advance of the baby's play or are overly interfering. Young children will balk at such unwelcome interventions. Even worse, the parents are creating a situation in which the children will not have the confidence to try things on their own. The best approach is to not get annoyed, not change the theme of the play, and not add anything into the play; instead, sit there being attentive and observant, comment every now and then, and be sure to give the child enough time to respond. Children are not as quick to reply as we might expect, but given enough time, most will respond—either through vocalization or action or both.

When to provide support

We have to ask ourselves what we can expect our child to do alone and when should we step in to help him with his problems and difficulties. We have to know when we should handle the difficulty for him and when we can help him to deal with it with himself. This means that we need to create the kind of relationship in which we let the child test his own resources, competencies, and strengths. To do this, the child needs to know that the parents not only care about what happens, but have confidence in his ability to do something on his own.

Example: Offering support

When Timmy started to walk around the coffee table, his parents cleared the route. They made the corners and edges of the table safe by putting soft plastic around the sharp edges. They put cushions in what they considered to be strategic spots and then they encouraged him to walk. Timmy's parents were ready to give him a chance to try things out, but they knew that they needed to make sure that he could do it safely.

Example: Interfering, and even damaging

Sasha was learning how to feed himself, but his parents did not have the time to let him do things for himself. They did not want him to be "too messy" and take too long to eat, so they usually fed him while he played with one of his toys. When he tried to grab for the food, they stopped his hands or made a face saying, "That's dirty" or "Don't touch." Soon Sasha stopped trying to interfere with his feedings and his parents thought that they were doing a good job because there was so much more time to play with him now that mealtimes were over so quickly. Unfortunately Sasha developed an eating problem. At first, he only wanted certain foods, like bananas. Then he went "off" bananas and only drank milk. He soon stopped drinking milk and would not eat at all. He simply closed his mouth and turned his head away from the spoon. This fifteen-month-old baby was reacting to his parents' demands that he eat quickly and cleanly by not eating at all. He may have had a point—it is much faster if you don't eat at all!

• • •

Babies need to try to feed themselves. They need to play with their food. Sometimes, they even need to try to feed their parents. They use their special spoons in ways that are spoon-like. At other times, they act as if they are not spoons, but combs to be run through their hair! There's no doubt that letting their babies do this creates more work for the parent, but those who do are less apt to have children with eating problems.

My philosophy about eating and play

I think there are times when a child should be allowed to dawdle over food, make a mess, or play with their food. When the parents are in a hurry, they need to know just how much they can rush the child without the event becoming fraught with tension. Parents can recognize signs that they've been rushing their children too much when the children refuse to try things, when they immediately balk at frustration, when they cry easily, or when they wait for things to be done for them. These are children who do not participate in "doing"; instead, they wait for their parents to do whatever is necessary. These children see themselves as "not capable" and quickly stop doing anything that makes them anxious. The anxiety is just too hard for them to endure and they feel safer behaving as if they cannot do whatever it is that is making them apprehensive.

Example: "There's no point in trying"

Four-year-old Lucy had been very interested in piling blocks one on top of another into many low piles and would spend hours doing this. The blocks often fell down, but Lucy was interested in choosing blocks, not in replacing them or rebuilding the pile—which is what her father wanted her to do. After a few days of his "interaction," Lucy stopped playing with the blocks. She gave up a favorite activity because it was too hard for her to cope with her father's interference.

Chapter Seven

About Children Who Grow Up with Time-in

Time-in parenting encourages children to take risks. Without the opportunity to take chances—and here I mean take chances within safe boundaries—then children's thinking and behavior will become repetitive and similar, lacking in individuality. Divergent thinking and problem-solving will not emerge and only a few children will dare to do something difficult or different from their friends.

I think that intelligence is made up of many different aspects and cannot simply be reduced to any one thing. If we stop children from taking risks and exploring, especially if they also have to operate under externally imposed standards and adult expectations too early, then we limit their intellectual development. And we shouldn't apply the same standards to children of different ages. Some children will manage to adjust to adult standards, but certainly not all. Age and emotional maturity will often determine who will be able to adjust and whether the cost of such adjustment is a self that does not take risks.

When expectations placed on them are so much more than

they can tolerate, children will worry that they are failing their parents. When children are told "No more of your lip," "No more of that saucy attitude," or "No more babyish ways" before they are capable of maintaining these standards, they become fearful of trying new strategies. They stick to solutions that worked in the past, and have some difficulty recognizing when a new approach is needed. When this happens, their creativity and problem-solving skills are limited. It is important that the adult finds some of their child's thinking and behavior to be of value and that they communicate this to the child. For example, a parent told his child, "Thank you for helping me put the vegetables and fruit away. When you want to put six apples in the bin at once, you might try carrying them over to the fridge in a bag, not loose in your arms." The parent acknowledges the value of the child's help, as well as the source of the problem when the apples spilled all over the kitchen floor.

Criticism without anger and resentment enables the child to understand the criticism in a way that will not limit her attempts at creating ingenious ways to do things.

Minimizing "meltdowns"

It is especially important that children have time-in when they cannot do things alone and/or cannot experience emotions alone. Young children need the added protection of their parents' confidence and competence, their strength, and their parenthood—their self—to help them through fleeting periods of distress or crisis. As the parent loans her strength, her child gains confidence. Rather than being "spoiled," as is so often predicted, the next time this child has overwhelming feelings or experiences difficult events, she will try to handle the situation herself. Her inner strength and optimism comes from knowing that she can go to her mother or father without feeling as if she has failed or disappointed them. She doesn't need to "fall apart" in attempting to meet or pass a standard for which she is not yet ready. The child's self is actually strengthened by her parent's presence. While she is with her parent, the child can take the risk of exploring her feelings (of failure) because the anxiety of "falling apart" is much reduced. Based on her previous experience, this child knows that her parent will not allow this to happen.

There is another very important gain that is made at the same time. By simply anticipating that "my parent will be there" or that "I can go to my parent," the child's stress level over a particular event is lowered. There is less fear of failing or disappointing (self or parent) since the child knows "that I can be with my parents; that makes me feel sufficiently strong to try by myself; I'm prepared to try." A sense of independence built on time-in with parents, on the willingness of parents to allow their child to depend upon them, enables the child to strive for independence.

Example: Matching anger with anger

Three-year-old Terry was busily kneading playdough with her twin sister and a visiting friend of the same age. Each girl had a different color of playdough and kept to a different section of the table. Their mothers chatted and kept an eye on the peaceful scene. Suddenly a piercing scream shattered the serenity of the moment and a pitched battle broke out over the use of a rolling pin. Terry's mother tried to umpire the scene and told Terry that the guest should be able to have the rolling pin first. This upset Terry so much that she flung the playdough and everything else on the table at the wall and proceeded to have a full-blown temper tantrum. Her reaction seemed out of proportion to what had been going on.

Terry's mother then took her by the arm and dragged her to her room, stating that Terry needed time to think over what she was doing and how she needed to share things with guests. In the meantime, Terry was yelling so hard that she didn't hear a word that her mother was saying. When she was put in her room, she sobbed so intensely that her whole body shook. She kept coming out of her room until finally her mother got the message: Terry did not, and could not, benefit from being by herself in her room.

She needed to be close to somebody, to be held by somebody, and to be told that she was safe. Whatever brought on the excessive tantrum evidently scared the "wits" out of her and being left on her own was even more scary because there was no one to help her. Once she had sat on her mother's lap for a while, almost forcing her mother to hold her tightly, the sobs became softer, then subsided, and Terry was able to re-join the others. She continued to keep an eye on her mother and it was about half an hour before she was able to relax and play as before.

$$\cdots$$

Terry needed, and was asking for, her mother's support to go through the extreme emotional reaction that she was experiencing. She needed a re-creation of her original attachment to her mother, including the security, warmth, smells, and touch of a safe mother. She needed the re-creation of being contained and made to feel safe from her intense feelings, even though neither she nor her mother really knew why these feelings were being expressed. Certainly, the last thing she needed was for her mother to be angry with her or to put her out of sight. When Terry was given the safety and support of time-in, she was gradually able to regain a sense of competence, of her own internal control.

However, whatever Terry had been feeling that lead to her "falling apart" was strong enough to take half an hour to subside. Sometimes, we not only fail to recognize the need that children have to be with adults, but we also don't recognize just how long it takes them to get over an upset and reestablish their inner equilibrium. During the time that Terry didn't feel able and competent to be alone, she needed the protection and warmth of her parent's strength, her mother's ego, to help her through a short, difficult period. When a child becomes so frightened or so upset that she cannot get through the time alone, she needs time-in with her parent to regain her usual composure.

Teaching through "loaning" our strength

"Loaning" our strength—our understanding, acceptance, and recognition that some feelings are too strong to endure alone—gives a child like Terry the confidence that, with help, she can get through a difficult period. The confidence that is gradually shared between child and parent helps the child accept the risk of trying to handle the difficult feelings on her own and reinforces the child's feeling that "I can try it on my own the next time." Rather than giving up and having a tantrum in the future, the child is more likely to try to handle the situation alone. And if the situation and the feelings are too difficult and too strong, then the child is more likely to ask her parent for some help—essentially for time-in.

Teaching empathy

Social development includes the ability to be sensitive to others, to empathize or "read" other people's feelings. I think that children will not be able to do this accurately unless parents are able to read their children's feelings accurately, sometimes by identifying strong feelings in their children and/or, when they can answer, by asking them how they feel. Parents also have to be honest about their own feelings when, in turn, their children ask them.

I have too often heard children who are unable to judge other people's feelings because whenever they said to their parents, "You're angry," the parents have denied it even though they actually were angry. These parents said that they did not think they should tell their children how angry they were because it might "frighten" the children. Sometimes they did not know themselves that they were angry. In general, these parents felt that their children did not need to know how they felt, they just needed to know what to do! The ability to predict and understand the feelings of others rests on important "others" telling you that you are right when you have accurately identified the emotion. Denying what is obvious to the child leads children to distrust their own judgments and, over time, to not even try to understand others or themselves. These children seem to go from reaction to reaction, as if looking for ways that they can "really" tell what's happening. So some of these children actually create events in order to cause a "blow-up" because then "you really know how to read your parents!" It's unfortunate that some children are driven to this extreme only to be told that they have to go into their rooms and stay there—until they learn that they're not allowed to recognize such intense feelings in their parents.

When "I know" really means "I don't know"

A four-year-old boy of my acquaintance would always say, "I know" to anything that was said or asked. He knew it all! When he was told the rules of a game, he said, "I know." When an event or a situation was described to him, he said, "I know that." He persisted with "I know" until he was asked a question about the sky and clouds. At that point, he very angrily said, "If you tell me, then I'll know!" When he was told the answer to the question, he said, "I knew that!" This young boy needed to already know everything. I think he was demonstrating his self-control by knowing everything. When he had a grip on his self-control, I didn't hear "I know" anymore!

In a similar way, babies about nine to twelve months begin to shake their heads, no, to just about everything their parents ask them or tell them. When they are being fed, they shake their head, no. When they are asked if they want a toy, even a favorite one, they shake their head, no. Parents variously describe this behavior as "strange," "cute," or as "I don't know what this means." I think this shows the very beginnings of self-control, in which the baby is trying to internalize the idea of no. The baby is saying no to himself, and is beginning to develop a sense not only of who he is, but what feelings need to be under his control. The idea that the baby cannot have everything he wants whenever he wants it is becoming part of himself. I don't mean that the baby doesn't want the food, or the toy; rather, he is practicing the idea of being able to have inner control later on. The child is developing a sense of self-control.

The development of self-control

Self-control is achieved gradually and is not something that we can arbitrarily impose on a child. In fact, it must come from within. Parents often worry that their children will not develop self-control and quickly enforce rules that they think will help them do so. They use time-out, thinking that being alone and being told to consider why they were "wrong" or "bad" helps children to develop self-control. Some children respond to this approach by thinking that they are so bad that nothing will ever save them. These children take on a self-control that is characterized by self-accusation and self-reproach: everything they do will be "no good," they will never be able to atone for all the "bad" things that they have done in the past, and their future will be bleak because they will never be worthy of the nurturing they so desperately need.

Example: "It's not about bedtime. It's about control"
Jessica thought that her bedtime was too early and she felt angry about it (as most children will). Going to bed, naturally,

became "a problem." She anxiously tries to make sure that all the things she wants to do and all the things she thinks need to be done before bedtime are completed. These things can rarely be done in time and eventually her parent accuses Jessica of "dawdling." This only increases the child's anxiety because, once again, she begins to feel angry and thinks that she is not supposed to have angry feelings. The cycle develops in a very repetitive, almost compulsive, pattern of finding things to do before going to sleep because going to sleep means lying in the dark and thinking about being a bad person. Soon, going to bed has become a routine to avoid. Jessica is not being "willful;" she is trying to avoid the feelings of badness that she knows she will have when she is alone. This is a child who has developed self-control and uses it to control very angry feelings. However, she experiences self-control as self-reproach because nothing that she has done has helped her to get over her anger.

• • •

Of course, not all children respond to their parents this way. Some tend to ignore their parents and have constant arguments with them about growing up and being able to look after themselves. Ultimately, self-control comes about as a very normal aspect of growing up in a supportive family environment and I see such "cheeky" children as having less difficulty with later overpowering feelings of self-reproach.

Example: Containing the emotions of a baby who can't sleep

When parents are able to see that their children's feelings are just too strong for the children to handle by themselves, they can help by becoming the "container" for these emotions for a little while. One nine-month-old child who was waking up once during the night to nurse began to wake up two, and even three, times a night. Her parents wondered what was wrong and tried at first to respond the way that they had when she only woke up once.

However, the baby did not respond well to this same feeding pattern and soon the parents had to figure out something else to do. Nothing seemed to work, at least not for more than one evening. Together they decided that what was happening was that their baby was growing up and, in this new stage of development, didn't yet know what she needed or wanted at that moment. Rather than let her cry herself back to sleep, they would contain her sense of being uncomfortable by being with her, cuddling her, making her feel safe, and helping her go back to sleep. Their idea was a simple one. Their daughter was not able to cope with her sense of tension by herself, so they would be there for her when she needed them. They were tired for a few evenings, but, gradually, within a week, the baby resumed her usual sleeping pattern and did not wake up several times each night.

• • •

As I noted earlier, self-control is gained gradually and is not something that we can arbitrarily impose on a child. The way we respond to our children can result in different responses from them. Some children will be able to control themselves, some will blame all their problems on mommy, daddy, brother, or sister, and some will blame themselves for all their problems. Too much parental control at too early an age makes a child a worried child, one who may succumb to guilt or blame others. We can expect our children to accept self-control if we recognize their need to have some (age-appropriate) control while being able to accept some parental control. Parents, however, must set boundaries that are in keeping with the child's level of growth and maturity. Boundaries that are too strict limit a child's opportunities to explore. Boundaries that are too lenient force a child to search for boundaries and, often, to misbehave in order to find these limits.

By providing the child with our "supportive self," we create trust within our relationship. This trust nurtures the child's curiosity, his desire to take risks and explore. More importantly, this trust nurtures the child's capacity to recognize when things are not going well and when he needs help from his parent. It fosters the child's capacity to tolerate change because he knows that he can be with the adult if the situation gets too tough or too dangerous. This, in turn, means that the child can tolerate the idea of making a mistake without suffering rejection; instead, he will get help and support. When the adults give support and praise, the child then responds with more "grown-up" behavior.

The capacity to create "reverie"

It is very important to recognize that most children have the capacity to create a "reverie" for themselves. By this I mean a thought or a feeling of being kept safe by the parent. Children have sometimes told me that when they are upset, they think about times when, as younger children with a safe parent or safe, known adult, they were safe. It is like our three-year-old friend who said she felt safe and confident because she felt as though she had "her mommy in her pocket." A child's reverie can be thought of as an attempt to re-create the time when she did not have to handle all their difficulties herself. This reverie is essential for the development of self-control.

Children who are rejected by their parents or who are told to handle their problems on their own do not have this ability to think of themselves as safe. Rather they view the world as dangerous and their parents as difficult. The very children who get into so much trouble, then, do not have the capacity to work their way out of the problem by remembering, by imagining themselves to have been safe with accepting parents. These children, six-, seven-, eight-year-olds, have no recourse but to "try" their parents again, that is, to try to gain some sense of safety from them. But all too often, these children find that, once again, their parents are not there for them. These children, I think, will be those adolescents who will have to find some way to make themselves feel safe in their own minds. They will have to create a "reverie" that makes them feel that they can carry on, and all too often this reverie will be created by using drugs or alcohol, by being overly susceptible to peer pressure, or by joining gangs. I think that parents must create an adequate boundary for a child, an adequate container for the child's feelings. This is essential when the feelings are too powerful or intense for the child to experience by herself. If parents don't create this container, then the child needs to try to construct something outside herself to prevent massive anxiety from disintegrating her sense of self.

We all know of babies who go to pieces when they are undressed, or have their faces washed, or when their feedings are interrupted. These babies are restless, with a lot of uncoordinated movements of their limbs, and are crying or even screaming. When these babies are contained—that is, given a sponge bath that only exposes one part of their bodies at a time, or carried around in a comfortable and close way, or even fed while being held close to the parent—they respond with reduced distress and easier interactions with their parents. This containing on the part of the parent creates a feeling of coherence—a sense of being held together.

This time-in with our parents serves us throughout our lifetime. This feeling of being held by another, of being understood, of being thought about, of being contained, helps us when we are older whenever we need to have something—some thought or feeling—to hold onto while we are under stress. These time-ins enable us to reflect on—to have a reverie of—safe, contained times with a trusted, responsive adult. We can then approach our life problems with understanding and perspective.

Chapter Eight

Questions and Answers

The following are some of the most common questions that parents have asked me in my private practice.

Q. "Is time-in the same as quality time?"

I'm a working parent and I've read a lot about how important "quality time" is. What is the difference between "quality time" and "time-in"?

A. I'm not sure what you've read or heard about "quality time." It is often used to refer to the nature of the time parents spend in "face-to-face" interactions with their children, as opposed to the amount of time spent together doing chores or other household activities.

"Time-in" is most certainly "quality time." It is a parenting strategy and style for helping children who are experiencing episodes of emotional, behavioral, or developmental stress by staying with them while you resolve the feelings together. It encompasses the feelings and behaviors parents express when their children are "out-of-control."

Quality time is being there when your child needs you—even if he doesn't know that he needs you. So often, parents plan an outing, say to the park, which they anticipate will be pleasurable. To their dismay, their child might not want to leave the swings to feed the ducks, or hurls the apple juice out of the stroller, or screams because there is mud on his shoes. The parent feels that the "quality time" has been spoiled and takes the child home in disappointment and anger.

Taking time-in to resolve those moments of fussing on outings allows both parents and children to carry on with the excursion without feeling that it has been "spoiled." Time-in is practicable anywhere, anytime. Time-in parents recognize that their child's moods and needs will not adapt to the parents' agendas. The reality is that children will have moments of difficulty regardless of how much fun they are having—in fact, maybe, because of it! Children react with strong emotions to their parents' expectations and feelings—whether or not the parents have expressed them—and special occasions and holidays can often be both stressful and pleasurable for the whole family.

Q. "Help! Time-in isn't working with my three-year-old!"

I have a three-year-old daughter who gets out of control when she can't have her own way. This is an especially difficult problem when the things she wants to do are too hard for her, like tying her shoe laces or pouring a drink from a full pitcher. I have tried time-in by talking to her and telling her that she can't always do what she wants, rather than sending her to her room, but she just seems to get angrier and starts to hit me and yell.

A. You are to be commended for not sending your daughter to her room when she is angry with you and for trying to help her sort out what she can and cannot do. This is a confusing and difficult task for children of this age, who often have very strong and clear ideas about their wants and abilities. An important part of time-in is the way you respond to her need to explore her sense of herself. It might be helpful to ask yourself whether the things she wants to try are really unreasonable, or otherwise unacceptable to you, and whether you have helped her to understand this at a time when she is not upset.

If you are content that both of you understand the "rules," then quietly sit with her when you have to say no to a demand and she becomes angry with you. I would suggest that you tell her that you are very proud of the many things she can do—perhaps remind her of some of them—and recognize her anger and frustration at you and at the limitations you are imposing. Perhaps you could suggest an alternate activity, or talk with her about other ways she might do the thing—as you understand it—that she wants to do. By giving her a chance to explain her demands, you might find that she has something entirely different in mind from what you thought.

It is important not to "be angry" through body language or tone of voice when having time-in with your child. If you seem irritated or frustrated, she will react to your manner, even if you say that you're not angry. When children are upset, angry words or behaviors will trigger more anger and guilt in them. Even sitting too close to them, or talking too much, can also be problematic for some children.

Testing abilities against wishes and limits is a task that continues throughout childhood and into adolescence. Children will do this repeatedly as they grow, and as you change your rules and expectations to conform with changes in them. Constantly renegotiating this is a built-in way of ensuring that parent and child remain up to date with each other. Using time-in to discover creative solutions that suit both you and your child will stand you in good stead in the coming years.

Q. "…but they use time-out at school."

I have a five-year-old child who goes to day care in the afternoons after morning kindergarten. The workers in the center are always using "time-out" with my son because they say he won't listen to them and runs around without stopping. I don't like this because it upsets him, yet I see them using it all the time with him and with the other kids. The teachers in his morning program don't seem to have these problems with him. What can I do?

A. It is regrettable that time-out is so widely used as a solution to behavioral problems in some childcare facilities. I think that it is important for you to discuss this issue with the staff, pointing out that there seems to be a difference between his behavior in the morning and the afternoon. You may also want to observe in the day care for a time to sort this out before asking for a meeting to share your concerns. He may be tired after a half day of kindergarten, or perhaps the routines and expectations are very different between morning and afternoon programs. I think he is reacting to the use of time-out in the afternoon, and his "excessive" running is an expression of his anger and anxiety created by the use of time-out.

Q. "Is it too late to start?"

My children are ten and twelve years old and I am interested in what you have said about time-in. I find your suggestions very appealing, but I'm afraid that it is too late to start. They're almost teenagers and everyone tells me that teens don't talk to their parents, no matter what you do. Won't they think it's odd if I try and talk to them now when there is a problem, whereas before I might have sent them to their rooms?

A. It's not too late—it's never too late! In fact, if you use time-in as your children approach adolescence, you will be able to set a pattern for a different way of relating that you will all find useful in the coming years. Despite the advice of your friends, many teens and their parents continue to talk openly during this time. When you feel as if you want to send a child off to her room, instead, invite the "offending" child to pull up a chair beside you. Talk calmly about what you see, how you feel, and how you imagine your child might be feeling. Give her lots of opportunities to correct your perceptions and to share her feelings and thoughts with you.

Don't be surprised if your efforts are rebuffed at first—this will be new behavior for both of you, and your children may want to test out whether you will stay with them, or whether you're going to use time-out anyway. You may even hear sarcastic remarks like "What do you care" or "None of your business." This is normal and does not mean that your children are rude—they merely want to understand the new situation. Pre-teens and teens also often express themselves in ways that seem designed to provoke their parents. Their feelings are very intense and they are practicing expressing them. If you can remain calm in crises, and use time-in, you'll find that your children will soon create other opportunities to communicate with you, building on the confidence they will have gained through time-in.

When your children reach puberty, and even in the few years before, you may notice that, at times, they seem more withdrawn and less willing to talk to you. That is why it is even more important to take time-in during periods of emotional upset, offering them every opportunity to let you know how they are feeling and what's on their mind. If they are sent to their room too many times, then eventually you may not be able to get them out when you want to.

Adolescents, as much as younger children, need their parents' acceptance and understanding of their feelings and their moods. They are experiencing overwhelming emotions and impulses that are frightening to them and your presence will reassure them that you are not scared and they are not "falling apart." They also need your help to develop a vocabulary to express themselves, and the example you set during time-in is important in allowing this to emerge.

However, most children, including teens, react badly to what they feel is an interrogation or being "put on the spot." It is often helpful when having time-in with a teenager to do something together while you talk, such as preparing dinner or going for a walk. This lessens the likelihood that they will feel confronted. They also need time to think about their reactions, and may come back to you with thoughts or comments when you least expect it. Teens need a lot of space and time-in can be effective even if you only stay within earshot and allow them to approach you when they feel ready.

Q. "We don't have time to use time-in!"

My husband and I are at our wits end trying to deal with our four-year-old daughter who screams and has a lot of tantrums, day and night, no matter what we do. She wakes up crabby, fusses about what to eat, what to wear, and every little change and task seems to precipitate a crisis. We've tried being predictable and consistent. We've tried talking to her in advance of situations. We've tried everything, but she is just so "high energy" and "high need" that we're worn out. The only thing that seems to work in terms of getting her to do what she has to do as part of normal routines is time-out.

If we have to take more time with her as time-in, then we'll never get dinner made, or get out the door in the morning, and our older daughter will be completely neglected. As it is, she doesn't get as much help with her homework or as much attention as she needs. What can we do?

A. You've obviously been trying very hard to meet the needs of both of your children, with only some limited success. As you have pointed out, your younger daughter's behavior has not really changed over the long term, despite the "effectiveness" of the time-outs. That is often the case with punishments like time-out or spanking—the effects are only very temporary because the child's feelings of rejection and abandonment are so powerful that she often alters her behavior quickly and dramatically. Nevertheless, the original emotions have not been dealt with and new feelings of anger have been added with each use of time-out, leading to a spiral of repeated episodes of difficult behaviors.

I would encourage you both to have a time-in with your daughter, even if you feel frustrated and tired. I think that you will find that you will not be spending excess amounts of time after the first few successful time-ins because your daughter will settle down as she anticipates your availability to soothe her emotions in a crisis. You will need to help her less frequently as she feels loved and accepted by you in crises.

Even managing time-outs is time-consuming and disruptive, and the feelings of rejection and anger that your daughter is left with as a result of the time-outs may even be provoking some of the outbursts the next day.

Q. "What if my child tells me to 'Go away!'?"

What if my child tells me to 'go away!' or to "leave him alone" when he is having a tantrum? I've always thought that I should respect his wishes. What do I do?

A. I'm not sure how you and your son have handled tantrums in the past and what he expects you to say or do when he is having a tantrum. It is possible to stay nearby, perhaps sitting near him on the floor, or just outside the door, talking gently to him even though he doesn't seem to be listening to you. You can respect his wishes not to be "too close" by having time-in nearby, even if you are not sitting side by side. I would encourage you not to leave him completely alone despite his statements. He may just be worrying about how damaging his angry thoughts and feelings could be to you, or whether you could still love such an upset child.

What is important is that you present yourself to him in a way that he experiences as accepting and non-judgmental. It may help to reassure him that you are not angry or upset with him for his tantrum, nor are you offended at being "sent away." You may have to "sit it out" with him a few times before he stops testing whether you think he is so bad that he doesn't "deserve" to have you stay with him.

Q. "How do I do time-in when I have to go out?"

I have a five-year-old girl who "goes crazy" every time I go out and she has to stay with a babysitter. She seems happy and well adjusted at other times and goes to school easily. It's getting to the point where I dread going out because of the fuss. I've tried talking to her the day before to prepare her, but this doesn't seem to help. She either ignores me or promises to be good when I go the next day, only to "melt down" anyway. The problem is, I can't take time-in with her at that moment because I am on my way out, and I don't want to be late. What should I do?

A. It sounds as if you have started to try a time-in strategy by talking with your daughter before you go out, and this is a very good idea. Perhaps the two of you can set aside some special time to be together for fifteen or so minutes before you start getting ready to go out. You might allow her to stay with you while you are getting dressed, maybe even helping you select clothes. Talk to her while you're getting ready about where you will be going, who will be taking care of her, and when you will return. You may also want to suggest that she draw a picture for you, to be waiting for you on your return.

If she begins to get agitated during this time-in, you can hug her and tell her that you love her, and that both of you will be safe while you're away. You can reassure her that, although you'll be enjoying yourself while you are out, you will also be thinking about her, and that it is okay for her to have fun as well.

She may still create a "scene" at the door and it might be a good idea to allow five or so minutes for this in your scheduling. Again, you can hold her and tell her that you'll both be okay, and that you will return when she is asleep, or whatever suits the time of day. With your support in these time-ins, she will gradually be able to manage the strong feelings she has when you leave her.

Q. "I give toys time-out, not kids!"

I really agree with your suggestions about time-in. I have never liked time-out for kids, but our family has used it for a toy instead! If my kids cannot agree to share, I put the toy in time-out until they have a plan that they both agree on for playing with it. What is your reaction to this idea?

A. You are to be congratulated for not using time-out with your children. I do think that expecting your children to agree on how to share a toy before playing with it can be useful for developing cooperative skills, depending on the ages of the children. I would, however, avoid putting the toy in time-out. The children will think the toy is "bad" and therefore has been rejected. It does not require a large leap of imagination for your children to put themselves in the place of the toy, and, in their minds, they may be worried that they will be next.

Q. "How do I give time-in when I'm exhausted after work?"

When I come home from work I look forward to seeing my kids, but they seem to erupt into fighting and misbehavior as soon as I come through the door. I'm also tired and want a little space to change my clothes and settle in. I know everyone is hungry and needy, but time-in is the last thing I feel like having at that moment. Any suggestions?

A. I think that what you and your children are experiencing is very normal and common to many families. You are indeed right that everyone is tired, hungry, and "on the edge." There are no easy solutions for this time of day. However, you can be certain that using time-out will make things worse. Children, understandably, want as much as they can get from their parents, especially after a long day apart. Parents want a little peace and quiet, too!

It may be that you will get a lot by giving a little. By having an immediate and focused time-in when you enter the house, the children will sense that you can, and will, be available to them, and you can absorb all of their immediate feelings. Then other issues can be dealt with as the evening progresses. The more you "fend them off," the more anxious and angry they will likely become.

It will be helpful for you to "fortify" yourself to do this by taking a few minutes for yourself before you get home, perhaps by having a cup of tea at a corner cafe. It will also help to tell the kids, while you are having time-in with them, that you are glad to be home with them, and that you are home for the evening (if, indeed, you are). They will begin to develop a sense of confidence in your availability for them in those opening moments and throughout the evening, and their tensions will quickly subside. By the way, have a small snack prepared for the children that you can bring in during the time-in.

Q. "My daughter does dangerous things. Shouldn't I punish her?"

My five-year-old daughter just wants to do dangerous things—she climbs onto fences and walks along them as if she's on a tightrope. Just yesterday she climbed a telephone pole and then couldn't get down. I had to get the fire department to get her down. I've punished her by taking away privileges, by spanking her, and by sending her to her room as a further consequence to let her know that she's doing some bad things. Nothing seems to work—what do you suggest?

A. You might want to enroll your daughter in a gym class where climbing ropes, walking, balancing, and other skills are taught. She may have a talent in that direction. Nevertheless, apart from enrolling her in a class, it does sound as though she needs to be active and may, in fact, need more of your direction, caring, and support on the spot! She might need you to help her recognize what is dangerous and what she can do safely.

Sending her to her room as a consequence of her behavior is not going to help her at all. In fact, it may only create a sense of anger and rejection in her. When she is sent to her room, I'm sure that she doesn't think that she has been bad, even if you told her that—nor would a five-year-old think that her mother was right to send her to her room to teach her not to do a bad deed. I have never spoken to a child who has been put in her room who has said, "Mommy and Daddy put me in my room because they love me." Rather, these children have expressed resentment and do consider how to "get even." I think that these retaliation thoughts leave children with feelings of guilt and worry that their parents will punish them for these thoughts—not for the original reasons that they were sent to their rooms. I think that children will behave badly later on in ways that seem unrelated to the original misbehavior because of the feelings they have when they are punished by time-out.

With time-in, you will talk to your child, telling her why she needs to be with you, why her behavior is dangerous, and that she needs your support right now. Often the misbehavior is an attempt on the child's part to ask for your time, your support, and your confidence in knowing how to handle difficult situations. The child's time with you reinforces the strength of the bond and enables her to call on you when she needs you. The time-in leaves you both with good feelings towards each other.

Q. "My eleven-year-old is out of control…How can I use time-in?"

My eleven-year-old son has been misbehaving in class—he has suddenly become the class clown and doesn't seem to know when to stop his nonsense. We have tried to punish him by grounding him, but that doesn't work. We know, and he knows, that the school is about to suspend him from class. Is there anything we can do to help him?

A. Yes, I think there is. You might try talking with him about his behavior. Tell him that you are aware that it started recently and you don't know why he's doing this. Let him know that you want to be able to talk with him rather than punish him—and you might find that going for a drive in the car, just the two of you, may make it easier for him to talk with you.

Punishing him won't work, as you are finding out. I think that he feels angry, sad, resentful, or humiliated and doesn't actually feel remorse or think about how to make the changes that his parents and teachers would like to see happening. Grounding him or giving him time-out carries with it the expectation that he "will know better next time"—but it doesn't have that effect. My experience shows that it is more likely to make someone believe that the person who imposed the time-out doesn't like him, and your son's clowning in class may be his way of trying to actually hide his anxiety at being rejected and feeling angry. Punishment only reinforces the misbehavior, which may actually escalate, causing you to punish him even more.

I think you need to have more time with your son. Try to find out what is bothering him and try to look at the behavior from his point of view. He's trying to get something from the class; he's trying to become recognized; he's trying to find out what he can do to stand out and be seen as an individual. These may be some thoughts he has. Our job as parents is to create a time with our children in which they can feel comfortable, safe and free, loved, and supported, so that they can explore some thoughts about why they do what they do.

Q. "What's wrong with letting babies cry themselves to sleep?"

My baby is seven months old and won't go to sleep by himself. I have to be in the room until he falls asleep. I've been told that he needs to learn to fall asleep by himself, but if I'm not there he cries and cries and has even vomited because I didn't go to him. Is this okay?

A. No, I don't think it's okay. I would not advise you to let your seven-month-old cry himself to sleep or cry until he vomits. All that you will do is prove to him that you are unavailable when he needs you. In order for babies to go to sleep "alone," they need to build up confidence in themselves that they can sleep, and fall asleep, alone. In order to accomplish this, they need their parents. By being with him and not letting him cry, he will gain that sense of confidence through your presence. If he is sufficiently important to you, for you to stay with him, then he will be sufficiently important to himself. It is the confidence in having parents there when we need them that gives us confidence in ourselves.

So be there when he cries, have the same bedtime routine every night, don't excite him for at least an hour before you start the routine, and then, when you have him in bed and quiet, leave the room. If he cries, come back and talk soothingly to him. If he persists, then pick him up and walk around his room with him. Try to put him back into his crib again and, only if he is all right, leave the room. Of course, you've made sure that he's not cold, hungry, wet, uncomfortable, or sick, and, if you've checked all these, as well as any other possible problems, then leave. If he cries again, then repeat the soothing and walking until he settles to sleep. You will find that within a short time—sometimes a week—he'll go to sleep easily by himself.

What I am describing is essentially a time-in between you and your baby. If you leave him to "cry it out," especially when he is upset, you are imposing a time-out. I think that this only creates other problematic behaviors that will be worse for both of you than his difficulty going to sleep. As well, leaving him alone in time-out lays the groundwork for him to have a smaller capacity for enduring future frustrations. In effect, he will continue to feel that "If you let me down before, you'll let me down again." He will expect this to pattern to recur and will cry more readily because he hasn't ever learned how to tolerate frustration.

Q. "How can I use time-in in class to help a 'squirmer'?"

I've noticed that one of the students in my fourth-grade class squirms a lot in his seat, especially when he has to do a short study test or answer some written questions that I've given to the class. Is there some way I might help him to be able to sit quietly?

A. I think that the student is communicating to you, in body language, that he is uncomfortable—or at least, under some pressure in trying to write out the answers to your questions. When children squirm in their seats, I think that it is because they doubt their capacity to answer the questions. They may even begin to feel ill, with stomach aches or headaches.

Have the child come and sit beside you and read the question to you that is to be answered. What you are doing is helping him to focus on the work rather than on his anxiety. In my experience, I have seen children remain beside their teacher and begin to write their answers—without any squirming and physical discomfort. When the child begins to write, you can leave him to talk to another "squirmer."

The child's anxiety about doing well is just too great for him to endure alone. He needs you to act as his "container" by having time-in with him—to listen to his reading and then allow him to remain close to you as he begins to write his answers. At that point, he won't mind at all if you focus on another child. His anxiety will have been contained, and he will be able to go on with his work.

Q. "How do I use time-in to deal with sibling rivalry when a new baby arrives?"

My daughter is very jealous of her new baby sister and no matter what I do, I just can't stop her from trying to bite, scratch, or hit her. She looks at the baby with such anger that it frightens me and she's only three years old. I've sent her to her room when she acts like that, but she just comes back and does it again. What do you think I should do?

A. I don't think that you should send your older daughter to her room. That only strengthens her sense of being not wanted or rejected. You now have another daughter and sending your first to her room only reinforces her feeling of being replaced—of not being wanted. She didn't ask for a sister; she thought she was all you wanted or needed and now she has found out she was not enough! Just think about it—how would you feel if your husband brought home another wife? Of course, you'd be angry and jealous. You would feel that he doesn't care for you any more or that you weren't enough for him, didn't "do" enough for him. Either way, it would make you very angry.

Don't send her to her room. Do have her come and sit with you when she tries to hurt the baby or has hurt her. She needs to know you love and want to nurture her and that you have enough love and nurturing for both your children. Let her know that you know she's angry, but that you can't let her hurt the baby and that you will make things safe for both children. With time-in, you lend your daughter your support and take care of her jealousy, which she can't deal with by herself. She needs your strength at this time in her life.

Index

Index